The Godhead
Doctrine

Written by: Bryan Denlinger

The Godhead Doctrine

Copyright © 2022 by Bryan Denlinger

All Rights Reserved

Unless explicitly stated otherwise, all scripture quotations are from the King James Version.

Website: kingjamesvideoministries.com

First Edition

Paperback Edition

ISBN: 979-8-9855452-0-3

Table Of Contents

Preface

Dear Reader,

You will need three things in order to understand this book: Salvation, a King James Bible, and Prayer. Please bear with me while I explain all three things in greater detail.

First and foremost, is the need for you to have experienced the new birth. 1 Corinthians 2:14 plainly states that the, "...natural man receiveth not the things of the spirit of God, for they are foolishness unto him, neither can he know them, because they are spiritually discerned." If you are a lost philosopher trying to figure out what I am saying, then you should put this book down, and get your eternal salvation sorted out first, before you proceed.

The second requirement for understanding this book, is your need to look up ALL scripture references in a King James Bible, and no other! I have defended the KJV for many years, and I know all about the various Greek texts, different translations, and the issue of textual criticism. I will never be moved away from the KJV, because I have seen its amazing life-changing power over the years. The new versions change many vital scriptures, which are essential to a proper understanding of the Godhead doctrine. So, get a King James Bible, and have it ready, so you can look up the many scripture references, as you come to them in this book.

Finally, before you begin your studies, please spend some time in prayer. In James 1:5 the Bible says, "If any of you lack wisdom, let him ask of God, that giveth to all men liberally, and upbraideth not, and it shall be given him." It is God's Holy Spirit that will guide you into all truth, not me. Please test every word I write, and make sure it is inline with God's written word.

Introduction

I despise the Trinity, and also the bizarre god of Modalism. Why is that? Because I believe that Jesus is God. While this might sound like a simple statement, the implications are actually quite profound! Let us examine the phrase, "Jesus is God" in greater detail. I do not believe Jesus is "a" God. Saying this would mean that Jesus is merely one of three (or possibly more) Gods. That would contradict numerous scriptures which plainly state there is only ONE God.

I do not believe that Jesus is a "lesser" God. One must rely on philosophy to make the statement that Jesus is, "the second member of the Trinity", as this phrase appears nowhere in our King James Bible. Jesus Christ is not a created God, and he is not weaker in power than the Father and the Holy Spirit.

Now, of course, the Trinitarians will take certain scriptures out of context, that speak of the relationship between the body of God (Jesus) and the soul of God (the Father). They will intentionally use these misapplied scriptures to attack the Lord Jesus Christ. We will discuss this in later Chapters of this book.

Now let us return to the original statement that, "Jesus is God". If you believe this, then it would logically follow that every reference to God in the Bible, must be tied in some way to the person of Jesus Christ. The Judeo-Christian faith is Monotheistic. There can be only ONE person named "God". Not three different persons, all sharing a title, while claiming to be the same ONE God!

Before we continue, I feel it is necessary to define both the Trinitarian position, and also the Modalist position. Trinitarianism is a belief that there are three separate persons within what is called, "God" in scripture. The first is known as, "God the Father". The second member of the Trinity is called, "God the Son". He came to the earth as, "Jesus Christ", and took on a body of flesh that was completely separate from both the Father and the Holy Spirit. The third member of the "Trinity" is known as, "God the Holy Spirit". He appeared as a dove, when Jesus was being baptized. All three persons are part of what the Bible calls, "God". They are not the same, but they all share part of the "divine essence" that makes up "God". This is the Trinity.

Modalism on the other hand, teaches no physical distinctions between the three names found in scripture. (Father, Son, and Holy Ghost) The only distinction is a spiritual one, where Jesus is on the earth, and Jesus in heaven is called the Father. In other words, when Jesus was walking on the earth, he was subjected to time and decay. At the same time, Jesus was also spiritually in heaven, and spoken of as the Father in his eternal state. The God of Modalism is not three different persons, but one person which manifests in three different ways. This is Modalism.

Now that we have an understanding of the two opposing views to the Godhead doctrine, we can begin to discuss the exact purpose of this book? Ultimately, it is to bring glory to the Lord Jesus Christ, and to put to silence the philosophical arguments against him. If you are saved, then this book will also give you a greater love and respect for Jesus.

There are three sections in this book, and a total of 21 Chapters. The first section will deal with Old Testament references to Jesus being the same person as God the Father. The second section will show proof from the New Testament. The third section will answer common attacks on the Godhead doctrine, from Trinitarians and Modalists.

This work is not intended to be an exhaustive volume which covers every single argument found in scripture. My desire is to encourage the reader to do further study on their own, and ask the

Holy Spirit to guide them into all truth. It must be remembered, however, that Satan (and his servants) will always throw more and more questions and doubts at a true child of God. Therefore, a basic and clear argument is often all that is necessary to establish the basis for sound doctrine.

So, with that as an introduction, let us now begin our study of the scriptures which relate to this very important topic. Please be sure to look up ALL of the references to various citations from the Bible, to see them for yourself. Your authority is the Bible alone, and not the traditions of men.

Section 1: Jesus Christ As God The Father In The Old Testament

Chapter 1: The Everlasting Father

Isaiah 9:6 For unto us a child is born, unto us **a son is** given: and the government shall be upon his shoulder: and his name shall be called Wonderful, Counseller, The mighty God, **The everlasting Father**, The Prince of Peace.

The above verse is one of the clearest in the entire King James Bible about who Jesus Christ truly is. He is both "a son" and the "everlasting Father". How is this possible? Can one man fulfill the two titles of "father and son" at the same time? Obviously, the answer is yes. Every married man, with children, holds both titles. Let me demonstrate this point. I, Bryan Denlinger, am the son of Mel, and the father of Oliver. I am NOT two different "persons". I am only one man, with different unique roles as both a father and a son. I do not ask my son for advice, and I do not tell my father to finish the food on his plate! I am in authority over my son, and submissive to my father.

The Trinitarians will, of course, loudly protest this and point out that in order for Jesus to be called both "Father and Son", he would have needed to give birth to himself. Therefore, they would conclude that God the Father MUST be a separate person from Jesus Christ. If you believe this, then you are in very serious error. God the Father "prepared" a body of flesh for the Lord Jesus. (See Hebrews 10:5) He did not lay carnally with the virgin Mary and produce a child the way that mortal men and women do. The fact is that Jesus had to be born from a woman's womb, in order for him to truly understand what his creation goes through. So when the Bible says that Jesus is both Father and Son, it is not perfectly represented by how we are all born.

Another objection which Trinitarians use to try and explain away what is CLEARLY written in Isaiah 9:6, is that Jesus is a different "Father" than God the "Father". They will claim that Jesus is the

"Father of Israel" or that Jesus was simply *called* the everlasting Father, but yet he somehow was not *really* God the Father. Either way, you have two Fathers! This ridiculous argument is easily destroyed by Ephesians 4:6, "One God and Father of all...." So much for there being TWO Fathers! It is amazing to me how far Trinitarians will go to tear down Jesus Christ. Now let us consider **1 Corinthians 8:6:**

> "But to us *there is but* one God, the Father, of whom *are* all things, and we in him; and one Lord Jesus Christ, by whom *are* all things, and we by him."

Let us interpret this verse according to what was revealed in Isaiah 9:6. It isn't that one plus one equals two. But rather that one times one equals ONE. Remember what I wrote earlier about how a married man with children can carry two titles: that of a father and a son. The same is seen here in 1 Corinthians 8:6. Notice also the difference between the two titles: God the Father is "OF whom" and "we IN him", whereas Jesus is "BY whom" and "we BY him". What does this mean? Simple. ALL things are OF God, but he created all things BY Jesus Christ. (See Ephesians 3:9 to confirm this.) It would be like an artist saying, "I put my heart and SOUL into this painting". Yet it was his PHYSICAL BODY that picked up the brush and made the beautiful painting. The work was OF his soul, but BY his body. Not TWO artists, but ONE! See how simple things can be when you believe the plain English of God's perfect written word?

Chapter 2: God Provides Himself A Lamb

Genesis 22:8 And Abraham said, My son, **God will provide himself a lamb** for a burnt offering: so they went both of them together.

Again we see an amazing verse which proves that Jesus Christ is God. The wording of this passage is VERY important, which is why I stressed the importance of reading only from the King James Bible in the Preface of this book. All of the Devil's counterfeit new versions will mess with the unique wording of Genesis 22:8. They will say things such as: "God will provide the lamb" (The Voice translation), "God doth provide for Himself the lamb" (Young's Literal Translation), "God himself will provide the lamb" (NIV), "God will provide for Himself the lamb" (NASB), "God will provide for Himself the lamb" (MEV), "God will see to it that there's a sheep" (The Message), "God will give us the lamb" (International Children's Bible), "God will provide the lamb" (CEV).

Our text reads, "God will provide HIMSELF a LAMB". What does this mean? Let me illustrate this point. A delivery shows up at my home, and my wife is outside at the time. The delivery man asks my wife if Mr. Denlinger is available to help with the package. She replies, "Please give me a minute to go get my husband, and then Bryan will provide HIMSELF to help move the heavy package." Would there be any doubt in the delivery man's mind about who was coming to help him? Of course not. He would be expecting to meet "Mr. Denlinger", and no one else. But what if my wife had said, "Bryan himself will provide someone to help you with the heavy package." Do you see how that changes the meaning entirely? Now, the delivery man might be expecting to see me, or perhaps an employee, or someone else. The KJV wording is the only one which lines up with the truth!

Before we move on, we need to consider the prophecy which was clearly given in Genesis 22:8. Did it come to pass? Was Jesus Christ both the "lamb" and "God himself"? Yes, he most certainly was. Turn in your King James Bible to **Acts 20:28**:

"Take heed therefore unto yourselves, and to all the flock, over the which the Holy Ghost hath made you overseers, to feed the church of God, which he hath purchased with his own blood."

This verse proves that God died on the cross and shed his blood, to purchase the church. The Trinitarian must look at this and say that it was NOT God the Father or God the Holy Ghost which died on the cross, but rather "God the Son". The problem with this interpretation is that there is not one verse of scripture which ever calls Jesus Christ, "God the Son". It creates a teaching with more than one God. They must enter into the realm of Philosophy (man's wisdom) to try and explain how three separate persons (each with a unique "God" title!) can actually share the singular title of "God". Apparently, the Trinity "Gods" like to pretend that they are just one God, when they secretly know they are three different beings. Funny how these "Gods" don't have a problem with lying, and cannot seem to handle simple arithmetic. Three separate things cannot be one single thing, unless you are talking about three parts composing ONE item.

Now let us consider two other verses:

John 1:29 The next day John seeth Jesus coming unto him, and saith, Behold the Lamb of God, which taketh away the sin of the world.

Revelation 5:6 And I beheld, and, lo, in the midst of the throne and of the four beasts, and in the midst of the elders, stood a Lamb as it had been slain, having seven horns and seven eyes, which are the seven Spirits of God sent forth into all the earth.

12

Revelation 5:7 And he came and took the book out of the right hand of him that sat upon the throne.

The passage in John Chapter 1 makes it very clear as to who the "Lamb of God" is. There is no debate that Jesus Christ fulfilled the prophecy spoken by Abraham in Genesis 22:8. I thank and praise my God and Saviour Jesus Christ for dying as a lamb, to take away my sins! What an amazing truth and promise for all those who have been truly born again. But, look at the unique situation which we will one day see in heaven, after the resurrection of the body of Christ. We will see a "Lamb" and "him that sat upon the throne". What appears to be two separate "persons". To a Trinitarian perhaps, but to those of us with more discernment, we can see the separation of the body and soul of the Godhead. The Father is on the throne, and the Son is the Lamb who takes the book out of the Father's hand. This passage destroys the bizarre shape-shifting "God" of Modalism. They cannot pull a "God in eternity" and "God in time" statement with this passage! Both Father and Son are present in heaven (eternity) at the exact same time, and are physically reacting to each other.

This of course brings up an interesting question: Can the soul and spirit and body act independently of each other? Yes. How do we know? Look at Revelation Chapter 6, verses 9-11. Here you will read about the 5th seal being opened, and how John sees the SOULS of the martyrs, and how PHYSICAL ROBES were given to them to wear. Here on earth we cannot see eternal souls, but in heaven (eternity) we will see them. Now think about that for a minute. Here on earth, no one was able to see the soul of God. The Father was NOT visible. The only thing people could see was the physical body of God, the Lord Jesus Christ. In heaven, we will see both the Father and the Son. But, wouldn't that mean they are separate "persons"? No. It means the body and soul of God can be separate. Just like the souls of the martyrs were temporarily separated from their bodies, and yet they wanted vengeance for their "blood" which was shed on the earth. Souls do not bleed! God's soul (the Father) did not bleed on the cross. God's body (Jesus) shed his blood for the remission of sins. It's just that simple.

Chapter 3: Beside Me There Is No Saviour

Isaiah 43:10 Ye are my witnesses, saith the LORD, and my servant whom I have chosen: that ye may know and believe me, and understand that I am he: before me there was no God formed, neither shall there be after me.
Isaiah 43:11 I, even I, am the LORD; and beside me there is no saviour.

See how the above verses tie in perfectly with what we learned in Chapter 2? The King James Bible teaches that there is only ONE God, not three separate persons with unique "God" titles. Always remember that "God the Father" is scriptural, "God the Son" and "God the Holy Ghost (or Spirit)" have no basis in scripture, and were added by Trinitarian philosophers. They must have three separate beings each claiming to be "God", because there is a future satanic counterfeit which will be worshiped as the "Trinity". (More on that later in this book)

Now, let us examine Isaiah 43:10-11 in more detail. Verse 10 clearly states that "the Lord" has chosen a "servant", and that you are to "know and believe" the Lord, and understand that the Lord (I am) is "he". Who is the "he"? In context it is talking about the "servant" which the Lord has chosen. So we have God the Father speaking about Jesus Christ, the "servant" which will be the Saviour of the world, so that we might be able to know the Lord. But the beautiful thing about this passage is that the Lord makes it clear that, "beside ME there is no saviour." God the Father could not die a PHYSICAL death for our sins, because he is an eternal soul. But Jesus the "servant" could take on a mortal body of flesh, and shed his blood to redeem us to himself. Did Jesus ever claim to be the "I am he" of Isaiah 43:10? Yes! Look at the following passage:

John 8:24 I said therefore unto you, that ye shall die in your sins: for if ye believe not that **I am he**, ye shall die in your sins.

Isn't it interesting that Jesus uses the exact words, "I am he" that appear in Isaiah 43:10, to the lost Pharisees who hated him, and refused to believe that he was God manifest in the flesh. Then later on in the Chapter in verse 58, Jesus tells them, "Before Abraham was, I am". Again Jesus makes it plain that he is God the Father, by using his title. And what was the reaction of the wicked Pharisees that heard him? They picked up stones, and tried to kill Jesus (verse 59). Funny how I have heard many Trinitarians today become just as angry when you say that Jesus and God the Father are one and the same being. It must be the same spirit leading the ancient Pharisees and the modern Trintarians. In fact this spirit will often manifest itself when a Trinitarian reads or tries to quote John 8:24. They will intentionally remove the word "he" from the statement which Jesus makes, thereby shortening "I am he" to simply "I am". By doing this, they are destroying the cross reference to Isaiah 43:10. Coincidence? I think not!

Chapter 4: Melchizedek

Genesis 14:18 And **Melchizedek** king of Salem brought forth bread and wine: and he was **the priest of the most high God.**

Now we have a passage in scripture which throws nearly all of the "scholars" into fits about the identity of this mysterious man named, "Melchizedek". The strange thing about this, is that the New Testament CLEARLY identifies who he is. Before we continue, I must say that the Hebrew spelling above of "Melchizedek" is translated from the Greek New Testament as, "Melchisedec". Now let's look at a few scriptures in the book of Hebrews:

Hebrews 5:5 So also **Christ** glorified not himself to be made an high priest; but he that said unto him, Thou art my Son, to day have I begotten thee.
Hebrews 5:6 As he saith also in another place, **Thou art a priest for ever after the order of Melchisedec.**

Hebrews 6:20 Whither the forerunner is for us entered, **even Jesus, made an high priest for ever after the order of Melchisedec.**

Could the scriptures be any clearer than this? Jesus Christ is the high priest known as Melchizedek in the Old Testament, and Melchisedec in the New Testament. So, why is there any debate over the identity of Melchizedek? The confusion comes in Hebrews Chapter 7. The verses we are about to look at, can only be explained by those who understand the Godhead doctrine. What you are about to read will not line up with either Trinitarianism or Modalism. Turn in your King James Bible and examine these verses for yourself:

Hebrews 7:1 For this **Melchisedec, king of Salem**, priest of the most high God, who met Abraham returning from the slaughter of the

kings, and blessed him;
Hebrews 7:2 To whom also Abraham gave a tenth part of all;
first being by interpretation King of righteousness, and after that also
King of Salem, which is, King of peace;

First, we need to notice how the verse starts: "For THIS
Melchisedec...". Chapter 7 verse 1 is being tied back to Chapter 6
verse 20, which named JESUS as Melchisedec. Secondly, we need to
realize that Hebrews 7:1 is referring to the event which took place in
Genesis 14:18. There is no doubt that Jesus physically appeared in the
Old Testament, to Abraham. (See John 8:56-59 for another amazing
tie-in to this event!) But the next verse is where the "problems" for
Trinitarians really begin:

Hebrews 7:3 Without father, without mother, without descent,
having neither beginning of days, nor end of life; but made like unto
the Son of God; abideth a priest continually.

Oh boy! Now comes the trouble. If this "Melchisedec" is Jesus,
how could he be "without father" and "without mother"? How could
Jesus have "neither beginning of days, nor end of life"? Didn't Jesus
DIE on the cross? Then it must be someone else, such as Shem or
perhaps an angel. No, because they do not fit either. And what about
the rest of verse 3 which states that he was "made like unto the Son of
God"? But some might say that the Son of God did not show up until
the New Testament recorded the birth of Jesus Christ. If that is what
you believe, then you must have missed Daniel 3:25 where
Nebuchadnezzar sees a fourth man in the burning fiery furnace, whose
form is "like the Son of God."

So, how does this work? Well, if you believe that God the Father
and Jesus the Son are two separate persons, then it will not work for
you. If on the other hand, you believe in the Godhead, then you will
have no problem interpreting Hebrews 7:1. Let's break the verse down,

by looking at the first two words: "without father". This is not true about the physical body of God, the Lord Jesus Christ. It IS true, however for the soul of the Godhead, namely, God the Father. He did not have a father, and he did not have a mother. He also did not have "beginning of days, nor end of life". When God the Father was "made like unto the Son of God", he was inside of the physical body of Jesus as he walked around on the earth. Don't believe me? A bit too much to handle? Then please explain the following verses of scripture:

> **Leviticus 26:11** And I will set my tabernacle among you: and **my soul** shall not abhor you.
> **Leviticus 26:12** And **I will walk among you, and will be your God**, and ye shall be my people.

Please notice that the "soul" of God is what is being referred to here. This is a reference to the Father, which is obvious in the context of who was speaking in Leviticus. Verse 12 shows that God the Father gave a prophecy that he would one day, "walk among you, and will be your God..." Was this prophecy ever fulfilled, or is it yet to be fulfilled at some future date? Look at the next passage of scripture:

> **1 John 3:1** Behold, what manner of love **the Father** hath bestowed upon us, that we should be called the sons of God: therefore **the world knoweth us not, because it knew him not.**

Now in the New Testament, we have a reference to God walking on the earth, in the PAST tense: the world ("it") KNEW him not. Meaning that when Jesus was walking on the earth, the lost people of the world did not know that he was God the Father, in the person of Jesus Christ. (Soul inside of the physical body.) Still not convinced? Please examine these scriptures from the book of Romans:

> **Romans 1:20** For the **invisible things of him** from the creation of the world are clearly seen, being understood by the things that are

made, even **his eternal power and Godhead;** so that they are without excuse:

Romans 1:21 Because that, **when they knew God, they glorified him not as God,** neither were thankful; but became vain in their imaginations, and their foolish heart was darkened.

There were lost people on this earth that "KNEW God", and yet they would not give him the glory that he truly deserved. Who else but Jesus Christ could have fulfilled this? Nobody! So what is the conclusion? Jesus can function both as the Son of God, and also as God the Father in a bodily form which walked around on the earth, and talked to both the saved and the lost. Jesus IS God! Hebrews 7:1-3 can refer to God the Father, and Jesus Christ, at the very same time. It is so simple! The only way to miss this amazing revelation, is to try and force Trinitarian philosophy into Hebrews 7:3. THAT is why many "Bible scholars" cannot handle the text. They have been spoiled "through philosophy", exactly as Colossians 2:8 warns about! Now let us continue to read in Hebrews Chapter 7:

Verses 4-8 continue to tell how Melchisedec dealt with Abraham. Verses 9-10 speak about Levi, and how he was still in the "loins" of his father, when Melchisedec met Abraham. In other words, Levi was not born yet. Verse 11 speaks of the priestly class which came from Levi, and why there should be another priest. Verses 12-17 show that Melchisedec is a priest from the tribe of Juda, and therefore not a Levite. (Compare this to Jesus being called the "Lion of the tribe of Juda" in Revelation 5:5.) Verses 18-22 go on to discuss why the priesthood needed to change, and the fact that Jesus brought in a, "better testament" in verse 22. Verses 23-24 compare Jesus to the Levitical priesthood, and show that Jesus did not die the same way that the mortal priests of the Old Testament did.

Now look at Hebrews 7:24-25: Jesus has an "unchangeable priesthood". He was Melchizedek in the Old Testament when he physically appeared to Abraham. He was Melchisedec when he brought in the New Testament. (Read Hebrews 9:8-28) And, Jesus is still Melchisedec to this very day. He oversees the salvation of men's souls in heaven, by making intercession for us. (Compare this to 1 Timothy 2:5) But, perhaps you are thinking, "I thought Romans 8:26-28 says that it is the Holy Spirit that makes intercession for the saints." If you thought this, you are absolutely correct. Romans 8:26 clearly states that, "...the Spirit itself maketh intercession for us..." But, now we need to look at this verse:

Romans 8:34 Who is he that condemneth? It is **Christ** that died, yea rather, that is risen again, who is even at the right hand of God, **who also maketh intercession for us**.

So Hebrews 7:24-25 and Romans 8:34 both identify Jesus as the one who makes intercession for us, but Romans 8:26-28 identifies the Holy Spirit as the one who makes intercession. How can this be: Jesus and the Holy Spirit are both in the Godhead. So no contradiction. In the Trinity belief system, Jesus is a separate person than the Holy Spirit; so that makes a real problem for them! It also gives Modalists a problem, because Jesus and the Spirit would both be present making intercession in eternity, at the same time. This does not work for their system, either! Again, another proof that the Godhead doctrine is the ONLY acceptable way to interpret Hebrews Chapter 7. Verses 26-28 go on to further confirm that Jesus is Melchisedec, the priest of the most high God. Look at verse 26:

Hebrews 7:26 For **such an high priest became us**, who is holy, harmless, undefiled, separate from sinners, and made higher than the heavens;

Jesus took upon himself the form of a servant (Philippians 2:5-11). He "became us", and yet lived without sinning. His death was a perfect sacrifice, and therefore does not need to be repeated. (So much for the

Roman Catholic Eucharistic perpetual sacrifice system!) Hebrews 7:27-28 confirm that there is no need for any system of constant sacrifices. Jesus paid it all, all to him I owe, sin had left a crimson stain, he washed it white as snow!

Chapter 5: Jacob Wrestles With God Face To Face

Genesis 32:24 And Jacob was left alone; and there **wrestled a man with him** until the breaking of the day.
Genesis 32:30 And Jacob called the name of the place Peniel: for **I have seen God face to face**, and my life is preserved.

The above passage of scripture contains the greatest feat of strength ever recorded. Not very many men can say that they physically wrestled God! It should serve as a great challenge to all saints when it comes to wanting God's blessing in our lives. While we do not have to wrestle God physically, it can be a real struggle to continue in prayer, until God blesses us with an answer. The desire to give up, and admit to defeat, can be very strong. Yet the Bible tells us that our prayers must be "effectual" and "fervent", and that this "availeth much". (See James 5:16)

So what does this account in Genesis 32 have to do with the Godhead doctrine? It absolutely destroys the concept of the Trinity. Let us examine what is written, and compare it to other scriptures. First, we must recognize that Jacob only wrestled with "A man". Not three "persons". (Please remember this. It will be very important later!) Secondly, we must realize that Jacob identifies this man as "God", and plainly says that he has "seen God face to face". But how does this compare with what is written in John 1:18?

John 1:18 No man hath seen God at any time; the only begotten Son, which is in the bosom of the Father, he hath declared him.

Was Jesus Christ lying? Did he forget about Jacob wrestling with

God face to face? Or perhaps Jacob was just confused, and God did not think to correct him? The answer is simple. Look at John 1:18 more closely: the verse says that Jesus (the only begotten Son) "hath declared him" (God the Father). Jacob was wrestling with the physical body of God, but God the Father was there inside the body as the soul. Jesus Christ is the "image of the INVISIBLE God", according to Colossians 1:12-15. We will be covering this issue in greater detail, later in this book. So, how does Genesis 32 destroy the concept of the Trinity? Let us take a look at a very unique passage in the book of Hosea:

Hosea 12:2 The LORD hath also a controversy with Judah, and will punish **Jacob** according to his ways; according to his doings will he recompense him.

Hosea 12:3 He took his brother by the heel in the womb, and **by his strength he had power with God**:

Hosea 12:4 Yea, he had power over the angel, and prevailed: he wept, and made supplication unto him: he found him *in* Bethel, and **there he spake with <u>us</u>;**

Hosea 12:5 Even the LORD God of hosts; the LORD *is* his memorial.

WOW! Get a hold of this one! Jacob in the context, had power with God in verse 3. Verse 4 says he wrestled with "the angel", which is an obvious reference to Jesus Christ, the angel of the Lord. (Covered in greater detail later in this book.) Jacob "prevailed", and made "supplication unto him". God granted Jacob's request for a blessing, and renamed Jacob as "Israel". But focus in on the word "us" at the end of verse 4. Who, or what is the "us" referring to? Genesis 32:24-30 only records two men being present: Jacob and God. There can be only one proper interpretation of Hosea 12:4: Jacob (he) spoke with the Godhead (us). In other words, God the Father was there as the soul, the Holy Ghost was there as the spirit, and Jacob wrestled with the physical body of God, the angel of the Lord, who later appeared on the earth as Jesus Christ. But why didn't he identify himself as "Jesus", when Jacob asked him for his name in Genesis 32:29? Because his name would be later revealed when he was born of Mary in the New Testament.

Now look again at Hosea Chapter 12:4-5. If you still have any doubt, please notice that verse 4 ends with, "...he spake with us". Verse 5 continues by saying, "Even the LORD God of hosts". The passage is crystal clear. The LORD God of hosts consists of more than one part: body, soul, and spirit. Three in one. That is the reason why the word "us" was used in Hosea 12:4. The most amazing truth of scripture, is that God is not afraid to interact with his creation. He is not a being that has "better things to do" than to waste time with mere mortals. He has walked among us. He took on a body of flesh, so he can know our pains and sorrows. Almighty God, the creator of the Universe, was mocked and ridiculed by the people he created. Yet, Jesus Christ is the most powerful being in existence.

And perhaps this is why the Trinitarian doctrine is so popular. The theologians want to imagine an all-powerful God that sits in heaven on his throne, and does not get his hands dirty. In their minds, Jesus Christ seemed too lowly and weak, to be on God the Father's level. So the scholars decided to make "God" into three separate "persons". This way, they do not have to relate as much to God manifest in the flesh, and they can avoid experiencing the fellowship of his sufferings. (Read Philippians 3:10) The scholars can be highly esteemed among men, and gain the respect of their intellectual peers. They can sit in their "ivory towers" and dispense their talents and insights to the "laity" who are willing to perform the right obeisance to the learned Doctors who safe guard the "greater mysteries". Unfortunately for them, in creating their own "God", they have knowingly rejected the Lord Jesus Christ!

Chapter 6: The Glory Of The Lord

Exodus 16:9 And Moses spake unto Aaron, Say unto all the congregation of the children of Israel, **Come near before the LORD**: for he hath heard your murmurings.
Exodus 16:10 And it came to pass, as Aaron spake unto the whole congregation of the children of Israel, that they looked toward the wilderness, and, behold, **the glory of the LORD appeared in the cloud**.

In this Chapter, we will be taking a very brief look into the subject of the glory of the Lord. This issue is far too big to cover in a small book such as this. Lord-willing, I will be covering the glory of the Lord at a later date, in a book dedicated to that subject alone. Before we begin looking at the scriptures, I want you to consider what the purpose of life is, for all of God's creation. Look at this verse in the book of Revelation:

> **Revelation 4:11** Thou art worthy, O Lord, to **receive glory** and honour and power: for thou hast created all things, and **for thy pleasure they are and were created**.

The greatest purpose for all (both saved and lost) things that are created, is to give God glory for all he has done. This is what brings him pleasure. Think long and hard about that. If God is in complete control, he can use the most wicked depraved sinner for his own glory. I have seen this many times in my life. It does not mean that the wicked are automatically saved when God uses them for his glory. It simply means that the Lord Jesus Christ controls everything and everyone. By him all things consist! (Read Colossians 1:12-17.) God gives all men a free will to do right or wrong, and to accept or reject his salvation. But God can use anyone or anything for his own glory.

Now let us examine Exodus 16:9-10, and other scriptures that pertain to this very important subject. We read in verse 9 that Moses tells the children of Israel to, "...Come near before the Lord." What do they see? The "glory of the Lord appeared in the cloud." Does the Bible mention this "cloud" anymore? Yes, it does.

Exodus 19:9 And **the LORD said unto Moses, Lo, I come unto thee in a thick cloud**, that the people may hear when I speak with thee, and believe thee for ever. And Moses told the words of the people unto the LORD.

Exodus 19:16 And it came to pass on the third day in the morning, that there were thunders and lightnings, and **a thick cloud upon the mount, and the voice of the trumpet exceeding loud**; so that all the people that was in the camp trembled.
Exodus 19:17 And Moses brought forth the people **out of the camp to meet with God**; and they stood at the nether part of the mount.

If you are a student of God's word, then I am sure the Holy Spirit is putting a lot of scripture references into your mind, that tie-in with the above three verses. Our King James Bible is an amazing book! But let us examine these verses from Exodus 19. Verse 9 records how the Lord promises to come in a "thick cloud", in three days' time. Verses 16-17 record when this event took place. Now (if you have not already seen this) there is a very deep and profound future prophecy which is referred to here in Exodus 19. Notice the "thick cloud" comes down to the mount, and the "voice" of the trumpet is heard by the people. What is the great significance of this? Look at the following passage:

1 Thessalonians 4:16 For the Lord himself shall descend from heaven with a shout, with the voice of the archangel, and with **the trump of God**: and the dead in Christ shall rise first:
1 Thessalonians 4:17 Then we which are alive and remain shall

be caught up together with them **in the clouds, to meet the Lord in the air**: and so shall we ever be with the Lord.

The "trump" of God is the VOICE that a trumpet makes. This is what Christians will hear, at the resurrection of the dead and living saints. (Read Revelation 4:1 where John hears a "voice" which sounds like "a trumpet talking with me".) Now notice that we are caught up into "the clouds, to meet the Lord in the air". Do you see the amazing tie-in to what happened in Exodus 19? I am sure you do, if you are born again. But are there any other places where the glory of God is associated with a cloud?

Turn in your Bible to the book of Mark Chapter 9. Begin reading at verse 2, and you will see the account of the mount of transfiguration. Notice in verse 3 that the raiment of Jesus became "exceeding white". This lines up perfectly with what the apostle Paul saw on the road to Damascus. The light of Jesus was so bright, that Paul (at the time known as "Saul") went blind for three days. (Read Acts 9:1-9) Now look at verse 7:

Mark 9:7 And there was **a cloud** that overshadowed them: and **a voice came out of the cloud**, saying, This is my beloved Son: hear him.

Here we see that God the Father speaks out of the cloud. This does not mean that the Father and the Son are two separate persons or beings. It simply means that both the soul, and the body of God can speak at the same time. (Refer back to Chapter 5, and to Hosea 12:4, where the Lord says that Jacob spake with "us".) Now let us turn back to Exodus Chapter 19, and take a look at verse 18:

Exodus 19:18 And mount Sinai was altogether on a **smoke, because the LORD descended upon it in fire: and the smoke thereof ascended as the smoke of a furnace**, and the whole mount quaked greatly.

Is there a contradiction here? Did God come down as a "cloud", or as "fire and smoke"? The simple answer is, that God was connected both to a cloud, and also to smoke and fire. Look at Exodus Chapter 13:

Exodus 13:21 And the LORD went before them by day in a pillar of a cloud, to lead them the way; and **by night in a pillar of fire**, to give them light; to go by day and night:
Exodus 13:22 He took not away the pillar of the cloud by day, nor the pillar of fire by night, from before the people.

So what is the significance of the fire and the smoke? Why is there a cloud by day, and the fire and smoke by night? I could go into a long description of how it was given as a reminder to the children of Israel, about the realities of heaven and hell. Heaven is for those who are of the day, and those who can be in the clouds with Jesus. Hell, on the other hand, is for those who walk in darkness, and the smoke of their torment ascends up forever and ever. (Revelation 14:11) But that is the subject of another book. For now, we will look at a few more references before moving on to Chapter 7.

Revelation 15:8 And the temple was filled with **smoke from the glory of God**, and from his power; and no man was able to enter into the temple, till the seven plagues of the seven angels were fulfilled.

Here we see a plain reference to, "...smoke from the glory of God." The anger of the Lord Jesus Christ is currently being built up, and the ultimate consummation of this fury, will be when the temple in heaven is filled with smoke, and the vials of God's wrath are poured out on this earth. This will be the worst time in history, and very few people will survive it. I find it ironic that the Jews rejected God in Exodus 20:18-21, the same way that they reject Jesus Christ today. The book of Revelation describes the events of the "time of Jacob's trouble" (Jeremiah 30:7), and makes it clear that the Lord must show his awesome power to convince the modern Jews that he was, and is, their Messiah. Look at this verse:

> **John 5:45** Do not think that I will accuse you to the Father: there is one that accuseth you, even Moses, in whom ye trust.
> **John 5:46** For had ye believed Moses, ye would have believed me: **for he wrote of me.**

My question for you is, when did Moses write about Jesus? Moses never mentioned Jesus by name, so what is Jesus referring to? Simple. The glory of the Lord, which the children of Israel saw with their own eyes, and rejected! They were doing the exact same thing to God in the New Testament. Think of all the miracles which the Lord showed to the Jews in the book of Exodus. Then think of all the miracles he showed them again, when he was here on the earth. Simply put: The Jews were without excuse! Now let us consider two more verses, which will convince even the most skeptical out there, that Jesus Christ is the Lord of glory.

> **James 2:1** My brethren, have not the faith of **our Lord Jesus Christ, the Lord of glory**, with respect of persons.

> **1 Corinthians 2:8** Which none of the princes of this world knew: for had they known it, they would not have **crucified the Lord of glory**.

> **2 Corinthians 4:6** For God, who commanded the light to shine out of darkness, hath shined in our hearts, to give the light of the knowledge of **the glory of God in the face of Jesus Christ.**

How about that. There are of course many verses we could turn to, but the fact is that only three verses are necessary to prove

30

conclusively that Jesus is the Lord of glory. Notice also that all three passages can only be applied to ONE being, and not to three persons. But, I truly love the wording in 2 Corinthians 4:6, because it clearly shows that Jesus Christ is the physical manifestation of God the Father. God's glory is literally seen in the FACE of Jesus Christ!

So, having seen the scriptures, I must ask you the reader a simple question: Do you REALLY believe that Jesus is God? Are you willing to give up your philosophical notions of the Trinity and Modalism? Neither of these systems can explain what we have been studying. If you want to be inline with the scriptures, and with Jesus Christ, then you MUST believe in the Godhead doctrine. There is no other option.

Chapter 7: Let Us Make Man In Our Image

Genesis 1:26 And God said, **Let us make man in our image, after our likeness**: and let them have dominion over the fish of the sea, and over the fowl of the air, and over the cattle, and over all the earth, and over every creeping thing that creepeth upon the earth.
Genesis 1:27 So **God created man in his own image, in the image of God created he him**; male and female created he them.

The two verses above, are often quoted to try and prove multiple persons in the Trinity. The idea here is that God the Father and God the Son (and possibly God the Holy Spirit, too!) are having a conversation in heaven about how to design the first man. Trinitarians never discuss if it is the Father, or the Son, which is doing all of the talking in verse 26. Modalists often try to say that God was speaking to angels in heaven, because there can never be two distinct manifestations of God in the same place at the same time. So which view is correct? Neither. The text does not say one thing about God speaking to angels, and they would have to look identical to God for the passage to make sense. So, we can throw out Modalism. Trinitarianism does not work either. Let me explain.

Take a good close look at the two verses. Let "US" (plural) make man in "our" (plural) "image" (singular). If God consisted of three separate persons, then the text would have to read, "Let us make man in our images". The Bible does not say that. Again, I need to remind you the reader of how Jacob wrestled with God, and the Bible says that Jacob spoke with "us". The Godhead can refer to itself as "us", and yet be just one person. That is the plain teaching of scripture.

Now let us look closer at verse 27. So "God" (singular) created man in "his own image" (singular), in the "image of God" (singular) created he him. How in the world can you get multiple persons out of verse 27? It is impossible! Another very interesting point is at the end of verse 27: "male and female (two separate persons!) created he THEM (plural). God purposefully writes in the singular when referring to himself, and then shows that two persons (namely Adam and Eve) are to be noted by the plural "them". The Holy Spirit knows exactly what to write in his inspired written word!

One final point I want to make is this: If man is made in the image of the Trinity, then where are your other "two persons"? Did God lie? Does he get three separate persons, but we are simply stuck with just one? How then could he claim to have created us in "his own image" and after his "likeness". The Trinitarians sure do have a strange God. He might be all-powerful, but he seems to have a problem telling the truth. Are you sure you have the right God?

We will be covering exactly what it means to be made in God's image, in a later Chapter of this book. My prayer is that you will see that the Trinity teaching is FAR from being an Orthodox position. Trinitarianism and Modalism are both filled with contradictions and errors, which are simply glossed over by saying that nobody can really understand the true composition of God, when you corner them with the truth of the Godhead doctrine. It really is a very simple, logical teaching, when you just believe God's word, without a need for the added philosophies of men.

Our God created man in his own image. God has a body, soul, and spirit. Three parts of one person. Man has a body, soul, and spirit. Three parts in one person. It is so very simple! So why do they purposefully cover up this truth? Because the Lord Jesus Christ destroyed their minds when he took on the form of a man and lived such a humble life. The scholars have never been able to recover! I can promise you that the Trinitarians and Modalists would have been among those yelling out that Jesus was guilty of blasphemy, and that he should be crucified, if they had been alive when Jesus walked the earth. They would have hated him back then, just as they hate God the Father in the person of Jesus Christ right now! Not much changes.

Section 2: Jesus Christ As God The Father In The New Testament

Chapter 8: The Book Of John

John 1:1 In the beginning was the Word, and the Word was with God, and **the Word was God**.
John 1:2 The same was in the beginning with God.
John 1:3 All things were made by him; and without him was not any thing made that was made.
John 1:4 In him was life; and the life was the light of men.

John 1:14 And **the Word was made flesh, and dwelt among us,** (and **we beheld his glory,** the glory as of the only begotten of the Father,) full of grace and truth.

What is the basic premise of this book? The belief that Jesus is God. Anything and everything which is written about God, must in some way apply to Jesus. What about references to God the Father? Those passages are referring to the soul of Jesus Christ. Remember, the only way for the Godhead to make sense, is if you understand the difference between the body, soul, and spirit. Every other teaching is heretical, because words and philosophies must be added to the scriptures, in order to make sense.

Now, please read the verses in John Chapter 1, and tell me how you can get a Trinity out of that? How are there (in context) two different "persons"? God the Father and God the Son? The "Word" was in the beginning. This lines up perfectly with John 1:3, where it says that "all things were made by him." Now think about this for a moment: If ALL things were made by the Word, and God the Father is a separate person, then that would logically mean that Jesus the Word made God the Father. How ridiculous! Or perhaps, God the Father is not included in the description of "all things"? Maybe he just stood off to the side, and watched as his Son created everything, except for himself? Such nonsense. Yet, this is what one has to do, if you depart from the plain teachings of scripture, and add the philosophies of man into the equation.

And how do we explain: "The Word was with God, and the Word was God." Simple. The body is with the soul, and they (the Word and God) are one God. Again, have you ever known anyone that made a difference between their body and their soul? I never have. My body, soul, and spirit are three separate things, but they all make up one man. John 1:14 goes on to speak about Jesus Christ, the Word of God. John later writes that they have SEEN and HANDLED the Word of God:

1 John 1:1 That which was from the beginning, which we have heard, which **we have seen** with our eyes, which we have looked upon, and **our hands have handled**, of **the Word** of life;

Obviously, Jesus Christ is the only one who fulfilled this verse. John knew Jesus personally. John didn't consider Jesus to be "a" God, or the second member of the Trinity. How do we know this? Because John never wrote this way! Whenever John wrote about Jesus, he always referred to him as "God". It really is that simple. Just believe what you are reading in plain English, and stop listening to anyone who tries to complicate the clear teaching on the deity of Jesus Christ. Now let us look at another passage in the book of John, where Jesus teaches that he is God the Father:

John 3:13 And no man hath ascended up to heaven, but he that came down from heaven, even **the Son of man which is in heaven.**

Why would Jesus say, "the Son of man which is IN heaven", when he was standing on the earth speaking to Nicodemus? I thought that God the Father was in heaven, and Jesus was on the earth, at this time? How then could Jesus claim to be in heaven and on the earth at the same time? Again, a major problem for the multiple "person"

Trinity, but no problem at all for those who believe in the Godhead doctrine. The body and soul are connected. One can be in heaven (soul) and on earth (body) at the same time. (Please study Ephesians 2:4-6)

Turn next to John Chapter 5, and start reading at verse 17. Notice that Jesus says, "My Father worketh hitherto, and I work." Look at the reaction of the Jews who hear him, in verse 18. The Jews "sought the more to kill him" because Jesus said that, "God was his Father, making himself equal with God." I guess the Jews of Jesus' day weren't Trinitarians. They understood that Jesus was claiming to be God the Father. They refused to believe Jesus, and that is why they wanted to kill him. Now look at verse 23 where Jesus makes the statement that, "all men should honour the Son, even as they honour the Father." Could it be any clearer? Jesus and the Father are the same being. They are not two different Gods. It is impossible to truly honour God the Father, if you do not hold the same level of honour for Jesus the Son. It would be like someone sending you a gift, that is only for your soul, and not for your body. That would make no sense!

But what about the distinctions between the Father and the Son? Doesn't that prove that they are two separate persons? No. The soul is distinct from the body. The soul is superior in the sense that it cannot die or feel pain. The flesh can become weak from lack of food, or sleep. The flesh eventually wears out and dies. It is corruptible. They are NOT the same as Modalism teaches. Again, please understand that there is distinction in the Godhead. God is not one being that shape shifts into other modes of operation. That is heresy, and easily proven wrong from the scriptures.

Now turn to John Chapter 6, and begin reading at verse 45. Jesus says to the people, "...And they shall be all taught of God. Every man therefore that hath heard, and hath learned of the Father, cometh unto me." The people hearing Jesus were the ones being "taught of God".

They "heard" God's voice, and they "learned of the Father", when they came to hear Jesus. Why? Because the soul of God was speaking through the Lord Jesus Christ. Now look at verse 46:

> **John 6:46** Not that any man hath seen the Father, save he which is of God, he hath seen the Father.

How does this work? The people had NOT seen the Father, unless they were of God, then they have seen the Father. In other words, many of the people gathered around to see Jesus did not believe that he was the Father, therefore this truth was hidden from them. But for those who knew and believed that Jesus was God the Father, then they could claim to have actually seen the being who is God the Father! I will show you an even greater proof of this in a few minutes, but for now let us examine another scripture from the book of John:

> **John 8:19** Then said they unto him, **Where is thy Father?** Jesus answered, **Ye neither know me, nor my Father: if ye had known me, ye should have known my Father also.**

Again, another crystal clear verse, that Trinitarians must reject in order for it to fit into their system. The Pharisees come to Jesus and asked where his Father is. Jesus did not point them to anyone but himself. "If ye had known ME, ye should have known my Father also." Jesus is clearly God the Father. That is why the lost Jews hated Jesus so very much. Now look at a very stern warning in verse 24:

> **John 8:24** I said therefore unto you, that ye shall die in your sins: for **if ye believe not that I am he, ye shall die in your sins.**

In context, Jesus is speaking about God the Father. Now, please think about the warning that Jesus just gave. If you refuse to believe that Jesus is God the Father (like the lost Jews were doing!) you will die in your sins. How is salvation possible when you reject the fact that

Jesus is almighty God, with no other Gods before or after him? How can Jesus be the author of eternal life, if he himself is NOT wholly, completely God? It makes no sense. The Pharisees were claiming to worship God, while rejecting God! How can someone claim to worship the soul, and yet reject the body of God? It is sheer madness.

Now, before we continue, I must warn you about a very sinister satanic spirit which I have seen multiple Trinitarians manifest. When they quote (in speech or in writing) John 8:24, they will purposely omit the word "he" from the statement which Jesus makes. In other words, they will take, "...if ye believe not that I am **he**", and shorten it to, "...if ye believe not that I am." I have seen this quite a few times. They must eliminate the fact that Jesus is saying that he is the Father. "I am HE" in context, is Jesus making himself into God the Father. They try to say that Jesus is comparing himself to God's title found in Exodus 3:14 where he states, "I AM THAT I AM". Yet, the funny thing is, even when they try to change the word of God by omitting the word "he", they are still using one of God the Father's titles, and applying it to Jesus Christ! There is simply no getting around the fact that Jesus is God the Father.

Now, let us move on to probably the clearest statement in the New Testament about Jesus and the Father being the same being. Turn in your King James Bible to John 14, and start reading at verse 6. Jesus names three things that he himself is: "The way, the truth, and the life." If God is three persons, why didn't Jesus say something such as, "Now my Father is the way, I Jesus am the truth, and the Holy Spirit is the life." Why would Jesus name three different things, and yet use a singular reference to himself, "I AM..."?

John 14:7 If ye had known me, ye should have known **my Father** also: and from henceforth ye know him, and **have seen him**.

Oh no! The Trinitarians must get very busy and quickly invent some special philosophical notions of "essence", or perhaps some other wonderful Greek pagan words to explain away the plain English of our text. Just read the verse for what it says: "If ye had known ME, ye should have known MY FATHER also." The Trinitarians loudly object, and say that Jesus was merely talking about relationships! If you know Jesus, then you will also understand what the Father is like, because they are similar but separate people...RIGHT? Can the Trinitarian philosophers pull it off? No, they cannot. Why? Because the rest of the verse shatters their system! Look at it: "...and from henceforth ye KNOW him, and have SEEN HIM." Where is the separate person which represents God the Father? Aren't the disciples only looking at Jesus? But thankfully, the Trinitarians have Phillip to represent them. Look at what he asks Jesus in the next verse:

John 14:8 Philip saith unto him, Lord, **shew us the Father, and it sufficeth us.**

Good job, Phillip. You should get the "Trinitarian of the Year" award. Nicely done! Jesus just made a plain statement to you, and you took it to be somehow an invitation to go and physically meet God the Father. Phillip needs to see the proof that God the Father is not the same as Jesus the Son, then he will be sufficed. How does Jesus answer him?

John 14:9 Jesus saith unto him, Have **I been so long time with you, and yet hast thou not known me,** Philip? **he that hath seen me hath seen the Father**; and how sayest thou then, Shew us the Father?

In the future, a young man travels to meet me. He is not sure what I look like, but he knows my address. He walks up and knocks on my door. I open the door and ask him what he wants. He looks at me and asks, "I am here looking for Bryan Denlinger. Do you know where I can find him?" I reply back, "He that hath seen me, hath seen Bryan Denlinger." The young man looks back at me, and says, "Thank you, sir, but I am looking for Bryan Denlinger. I know you just said that you are him, but I want to actually see Bryan Denlinger. So if you don't mind, Bryan Denlinger, could you please show me Bryan Denlinger?" At this point, I would have to ask the young man how long he has been crazy in the head, and if he needs a ride to the nearest padded room, with a free straight-jacket to wear! All joking aside, why would anyone read the plain words of Jesus Christ, and come away thinking that Jesus was NOT God the Father?

If the words of Jesus in John 14:9 are still not enough to convince a Trinitarian, then please read verse 10! Notice that Jesus says, "...the Father that dwelleth in me". God the Father is the soul of the Godhead. He is inside of Jesus. Therefore Jesus and the Father are one and the same being. If you still refuse to accept this, then please look at John 10:30:

John 10:30 I and my Father are one.

Now, watch a Trinitarian try to expound that verse without ADDING to the scriptures to change the plain meaning of the text! They cannot do it. Proverbs 30:6 seems to be very fitting here! There is one final thing in John 14, that we need to consider before moving on to the next Chapter. Look at these verses:

John 14:16 And I will pray the Father, and he shall give you another Comforter, that he may abide with you for ever;
John 14:17 Even the Spirit of truth; whom the world cannot receive, because it seeth him not, neither knoweth him: but ye know him; for he dwelleth with you, and shall be in you.
Now who could this "Spirit of truth" be? It is obviously a reference to the Holy Ghost. How do we know? Look at John 14:26:

John 14:26 But **the Comforter, which is the Holy Ghost**, whom the Father will send in my name, he shall teach you all things, and bring all things to your remembrance, whatsoever I have said unto you.

A simple comparison of the "Comforter" of John 14:16 and verse 26, shows that the Comforter is the Holy Ghost. Plain and simple, right? Yet, look at this statement which Jesus makes:

John 14:18 I will not leave you comfortless: **I will come to you.**

In context, Jesus is speaking about the Comforter of verse 16. Yet he says that, "I will come to you." What is the only solution to this? Jesus can speak as the Holy Ghost! Remember Hosea 12:4, when Jacob spake to "us", and the context was Jacob speaking to the Lord. That is what is happening here in John Chapter 14. Jesus speaks as God the Father, and also as the Holy Ghost. Why? Because Jesus is God. We are not to let the Trinitarians or the Modalists destroy our simple faith in what the Bible plainly says about Jesus Christ!

2 Corinthians 11:3 But I fear, lest by any means, as the serpent beguiled Eve through his subtilty, so your minds should be corrupted from **the simplicity that is in Christ**.
2 Corinthians 11:4 For **if he that cometh preacheth another Jesus**, whom we have not preached, or **if ye receive another spirit**, which ye have not received, or another gospel, which ye have not accepted, ye might well bear with him.

Chapter 9: By Him All Things Consist

Colossians 1:17 And he is before all things, and **by him all things consist.**

I already made a reference to this point, earlier in the book. But we need to cover it in greater detail. Turn in your King James Bible to Colossians Chapter 1. Start reading at verse 12, and you will see a reference to God the Father. Verse 13 tells us that the Father has "translated us into the kingdom of his dear Son". So, the context starts with the Father, and then goes to the Son. Verse 14 mentions the very important doctrine of the blood atonement. Many of the new versions (from the Vatican) actually remove the blood from verse 14! This is the reason that you need to read and believe only the King James Bible. All other English versions are corrupt. Now let us look at Colossians 1:15:

Colossians 1:15 Who is **the image of the invisible God**, the firstborn of every creature:

Jesus Christ is the "image of the invisible God." Jesus is the physical, visible body of God. The Father is the "invisible" soul of God. Now look at verse 16, and notice that Jesus is the one who created all things. We know that God the Father is "invisible" and "in heaven", so he would be included in the list of things which Jesus created, if you believe that Jesus and the Father are two separate persons. But the real issue for Trinitarians comes in verse 17:

Colossians 1:17 And he is before all things, and **by him all things consist**.

Now the Trinitarians have a very big problem. The context is still talking about Jesus Christ. But the scripture plainly states that by him (Jesus Christ) ALL things consist. Again, if the Father is a separate person, does it mean that he is on life support, and kept alive by the strength of his Son? What did God the Father (and the Holy Ghost) do, when Jesus died on the cross? How did they continue living, if all things consist by the life of Jesus Christ? It makes no sense, when you have three separate "persons" in God. But it makes perfect sense when you understand the Biblical Godhead.

Colossians 1:18 goes on to say that Jesus will have the preeminence in all things. I do not know of many Trintarians who believe that Jesus has the highest (preeminent) place in heaven. Most believe that God the Father has that distinction. This error comes in because of the multiple "person" argument within the Trinity teaching. Yet, when one understands the simple Bible doctrine of the Godhead, then it is easy to see how one being could create all things, and give life to everything, and how Jesus could have the preeminence, above his own soul and spirit. Jesus Christ bears the scars of his crucifixion on earth. It is Jesus who knows all about our pain. The Father and the Holy Ghost also played their part in our salvation, but not like the physical body of God.

Now, turn in your King James Bible to the book of 1 Timothy Chapter 6, and start reading at verse 14. Again, we can see the context is about, "...our Lord Jesus Christ." Now look at verse 15: The Bible says that, "...in his times he shall shew, who is the blessed and ONLY Potentate..." In other words, Jesus is the ONLY ruler in heaven. Not a problem for the Godhead doctrine, but a big problem for the Trinity. But verse 16 makes the problem even worse for Trinitarians. Notice the verse reads, "Who only hath immortality". The context is still Jesus Christ. Does this mean that God the Father and the Holy Ghost are one day going to die, because they are not immortal like Jesus? If you believe in three separate persons in the Trinity, then you would have to answer yes to this question...IF you are being honest. Unfortunately, most Trinitarians I have met through the years, will just invent more lies, until they are so badly tangled in their own deceitful web of philosophies, that they must pretend that their confusion actually proves that they are correct!

Now, look at the rest of verse 16: "...dwelling in the light which no man can approach unto, whom no man hath seen, nor can see..." Who is this referring to? Obviously, it is a reference to God the Father. He is the invisible soul that dwells inside Jesus. But look how the verse ends: "...to whom be honour and power everlasting. Amen." God the Father also deserves honour and power. But how does that work when Jesus is the one with the preeminence, the immortality, the one who created all things, and by whom all things consist? It does not seem like there would be any power left over for the separate person of God the Father! Again, not a problem when you believe that the Father, Son, and Holy Ghost are the same being. Please give up on the Trinity, if you have not already done so. It is a ridiculous philosophy, with no basis in scripture.

Chapter 10: Who Is In You?

2 Corinthians 13:5 Examine yourselves, whether ye be in the faith; prove your own selves. Know ye not your own selves, how that **Jesus Christ is in you**, except ye be reprobates?

Question: What happens to your body when God saves you? All Christians know that the Holy Ghost indwells your body at salvation, and helps you to turn from sin. This process is called "sanctification". This of course is true, but now that you understand the Godhead doctrine, would not that also mean that you would be connected to God the Father and Jesus the Son, as well as the Holy Ghost? Yes, that is precisely the case. But is there support in scripture for this?

Please examine 2 Corinthians 13:5 carefully. Paul is writing his second letter to the most carnal group of professing Christians in the first century. He is having some doubts about them, because of them turning to false prophets and other gospels. He instructs them to, "Examine yourselves, whether ye be in the faith...". In other words, Paul was saying that he was no longer able to judge if they were saved or lost, because of how carnal and wicked they had become. So the apostle Paul told them to examine themselves to see if their salvation was real or not. And what was the ultimate test for genuine saving faith? "Know ye not your own selves, how that Jesus Christ is in you...". Paul was asking them to examine their own lives, and to see if there was any evidence that Jesus Christ was in them, and manifesting himself to them. If they did not understand, then they were considered to be "reprobates". Let us look at another passage of scripture to confirm this:

> **Galatians 4:19** My little children, of whom I travail in birth again **until Christ be formed in you**,
> **Galatians 4:20** I desire to be present with you now, and to

change my voice; for **I stand in doubt of you.**

The problem with the church in Galatia was exactly the opposite of the one in Corinth. While the Corinthians were becoming carnal and wicked, the Galatians were becoming legalistic and trying to return to keeping the Old Testament laws to earn salvation. Paul rebuked both groups! But please take notice how Paul makes the statement, "...until Christ be formed in you...". I thought it was the Holy Spirit which indwells the life of a truly saved Christian? It is, but if you remember our earlier discussion from John Chapter 14, you will remember that Jesus promised to send the "Comforter, which is the Holy Ghost..." (John 14:26), and how Jesus also said, "I will not leave you comfortless: I will come to you" in John 14:18. Jesus and the Holy Ghost are the same being. Both are part of the Godhead.

Now I want you to turn in your King James Bible to the book of Romans Chapter 8, and we will begin reading at verse 1. We read that, "There is therefore now no condemnation to them which are in Christ Jesus, who walk not after the flesh, but after the Spirit." The next 8 verses discuss the differences between the flesh and the Spirit, and show the importance of living a sanctified life. But look at verse 9, and think of how it further proves the Godhead doctrine:

Romans 8:9 But ye are not in the flesh, but in the Spirit, if so be that **the Spirit of God** dwell in you. Now if any man have not **the Spirit of Christ**, he is none of his.

Now, how would a Trinitarian interpret this, if they were truly honest. Since God the Father and Jesus Christ are two separate persons, then they must have two separate "Spirits". But how does that line up with Ephesians 4:4, where the Bible plainly states, "There is one body, and one Spirit..." And we know that the "Spirit" in Romans 8:9 is referring to the Holy Spirit, because it is spelled with a capital letter "S" and now one that is lower case. So, is Romans 8:9 referring to the Father and the Son each having their own Spirit, or is it referring to the same Spirit that indwells the Godhead? I think by now, you should know the answer to that one!

Now, let us look at Romans 8:10. Please notice the unique wording, "...If Christ be in you..." I thought it was the Holy Spirit which indwells a Christian's body? It is! Jesus Christ and the Holy Spirit are both part of the Godhead. You cannot have one without the other. If you have the Holy Spirit in you, then you have Jesus Christ in you. What an amazing truth! But where does this leave God the Father? We have seen the proof that Jesus and the Holy Spirit are in a Christian, but does the Bible say anything about God the Father being "in" a Christian? Look at the verse below:

Ephesians 4:6 One God and **Father** of all, who is above all, and through all, and **in you all.**

And there you have it. God the Father is "in" every Christian. Now, if that does not make you feel safe, I do not know what would. When you are threatened by the lost world, please just remind yourself about your connection to the God of the Universe! Talk about having powerful "friends in high places"! All three parts of the Godhead are connected to you spiritually. Why should you fear anything that Satan or his children can think of doing to you? The Devil cannot take another breath, without our God's permission. Praise the Lord for that truth! Let us conclude this Chapter with one more verse:

1 Timothy 2:5 For there is one God, and **one mediator** between God and men, **the man Christ Jesus;**

I have heard of some people who find this verse confusing when studying the Godhead doctrine. They think, "Why do we need Jesus to be our mediator, if Jesus and God the Father are the same person"? Could this verse prove that they are actually two separate persons, as the

49

Trinity teaches? The answer is very simple. If you remember our study on Jesus being the high priest of Melchisedec, the Bible plainly teaches that Jesus makes intercession for us. Why? Because Jesus is the only part of the Godhead which knows the physical pain from living in a physical body. All parts of the Godhead are inside of a Christian, but Jesus is the only one who can truly relate to the physical suffering we go through on a daily basis. God the Father can relate to the spiritual struggles that our souls go through. And the Holy Spirit can show our spirit how to discern between truth and lies. We need every part of God to guide us and lead us through this life, until we finally are safe at home with our ONE God and Saviour, the Lord Jesus Christ.

Chapter 11: Spoiled By Philosophy

Colossians 2:8 Beware lest any man **spoil you through philosophy** and vain deceit, after the tradition of men, after the rudiments of the world, **and not after Christ.**

Many people are shocked when they learn that the Trinity is actually derived from the writings of ancient pagan philosophers. Most people think that while the word "Trinity" is not found in the King James Bible, certainly the concept is. Yet, as we have seen so far in this book, I have demonstrated that the Trinity has no basis in scripture, and that the idea of three separate persons all holding the title of God, is nothing more than a preposterous lie. Now, we will see the proof from pagan sources that the Trinity is from philosophers and not from the scriptures:

251 *"In order to articulate the dogma of the Trinity, the Church had to develop its own terminology with the help of certain notions of* ***philosophical origin****: "substance," "person" or "hypostasis," "relation," and so on. In doing this, she did not submit the faith to human wisdom, but gave a new and unprecedented meaning to these terms, which from then on would be used to signify an ineffable mystery, "infinitely beyond all that we can humanly understand."*

252 *The Church uses (I) the term "substance" (rendered also at times by "essence" or "nature") to designate the divine being in its unity, (II) the term* ***"person"*** *or "hypostasis" to designate the Father, Son, and Holy Spirit in the real distinction among them, and (III) the term "relation" to designate the fact that their distinction lies in the relationship of each to the others."*

(Catechism of the Catholic Church, Pages 74-75)

What you just read is straight out of the Roman Catholic church's official Catechism. They openly admit that the "Trinity" had to be developed outside of the Bible, by using "certain notions of philosophical origin". Notice how they admit to creating the words "essence" and "nature", and they also use the word "person" to identify each member of the Trinity. In other words, they use the word "persons" when referring to all three members of their Trinity. Isn't it strange that professing Christians are using the exact same wording, as the single most evil cult on the planet? Many are not aware of the fact that the Catholic church also has a Monastic order known as, "The Order of Trinitarians"!

Now, let us further examine Colossians 2:8. The verse starts off with a warning that a Christian can be "spoiled" by philosophy. Both the Trinity and Modalism, are man-made philosophies that spoil you when you start believing and promoting them. Why? Because neither system is based on the Bible. Both groups are either ignorantly, or knowingly, worshiping false gods. It amazes me how arrogant Trinitarians can be when confronted by the Godhead doctrine. They act like we are attacking the very foundation of Christianity, because we dare to cast doubt on the Trinity concept. (Ironically, the belief that the Trinity is the foundation of the faith, is also found in the Catechism, Page 69, and Number 234.) I find it strange that Trinitarians believe God would wait until AFTER the New Testament was completed, to supposedly reveal the Trinity to saved believers. Utter nonsense! If God waited until the second century to reveal the "Trinity" to Tertullian, than that means that none of the apostles ever heard the word "Trinity" while they were still alive.

Colossians 2:8 goes on to say that these philosophies are "vain deceit". This spells out the Trinity to a "T" (no pun intended!). Trinitarians believe that: *"God is in three persons. They are all God, but none of them are the same "person" as the others. The Father is not the Son, the Son is not the Holy Spirit, the Holy Spirit is not the Father. Three different "persons" do not mean three different "Gods", but the Trinity is composed of: 1. God the Father 2. God the Son 3.*

God the Holy Spirit." Do you see any "vain deceit" in that system? The whole concept of the Trinity is based on deceit. The system contradicts itself. When you point out the clear contradictions, you are labeled as a "heretick", and told that we are not supposed to understand the "Holy Trinity". My God is a God of truth. He would not create a system that makes no sense, and has no basis in scripture. Scrap the Trinity system!

And, how about the next phrase in Colossians 2:8, "...after the tradition of men..." We have already seen that the Trinity is purely based on Catholic church "traditions", and not on scripture. Modalism is also based on a peculiar teaching from Catholicism. We will be covering this in the next Chapter. Now let us see what Jesus thought about another group which elevated their "traditions of men" above the scriptures:

> **Matthew 15:1** Then came to Jesus scribes and Pharisees, which were of Jerusalem, saying,
> **Matthew 15:2** Why do thy disciples transgress the tradition of the elders? for they wash not their hands when they eat bread.
> **Matthew 15:3** But he answered and said unto them, Why do ye also transgress the commandment of God **by your tradition**?

Am I to believe that the Lord Jesus Christ would rebuke the Pharisees for their man-made traditions, while he was planning to reveal the most important doctrine of the Trinity, nearly 100 years AFTER the New Testament was completed? To say that is ridiculous, would be a great understatement! Again, we see that this Trinitarian philosophy also relates to the "rudiments of the world". A thorough study on this issue is beyond the scope of this book, but I will quickly say that the word "rudiment" is defined as, *"to furnish with first principles or rules; to ground; to settle in first principles"* (Webster's 1828 Dictionary). Colossians 2:8 is warning against man's philosophies. The "rudiments of the world", would be a reference to the very basic philosophies which men use to draw you away from

God's word. Statements such as, "We always have done it" or "A little bit doesn't hurt" or "We know when to quit", are all basic philosophies which can draw you into increasing levels of sin.

Now, notice the most important part of Colossians 2:8: "...and not after Christ." The philosophies of the lost world are always (100% of the time!) designed to take you away from the "simplicity that is in Christ..." (2 Corinthians 11:3) When you are drawn away into Trinitarian philosophy, it will pull you away from Jesus Christ. You will find yourself putting Jesus in second position to God the Father, and making excuses for certain statements which Jesus made, where he gave himself a bit too much power. You will find yourself repeating things such as: "Jesus was fully God, and yet fully human." Where does the King James Bible ever say that? The simple answer is: you will not find that statement in any part of the Bible. It is a man-made philosophy, just like "divine essence" and "God in three persons". Finally, let us look at the next verse in Colossians 2:

Colossians 2:9 For in **him** dwelleth all the fulness of the Godhead bodily.

Who is the "him" referring to? The last name found in the previous verse is "Christ", so that is who verse 9 is describing. All of the fulness of the Godhead (Father, Son, and Holy Spirit) dwells bodily in Jesus Christ. Three parts to one body. Everything relating to God, is found in Jesus Christ. One being. One person. One God. One Saviour. One way to heaven. Make sure you are going there when you die!

Chapter 12: The Similitude Of God

James 3:9 Therewith bless we God, even the Father; and therewith curse we **men, which are made after the similitude of God.**

Webster's 1828 Dictionary [K-Z]
similitude
SIMIL'ITUDE, n. *L. similitudo.*

1. Likeness; resemblance; likeness in nature, qualities of appearance; as similitude of substance. Let us make man in our image, man in our similitude. Fate some future bard shall join in sad similitude of griefs to mine.

This Chapter should be a very simple one, but when it comes to Trinitarians and Modalists, old "philosophies" die hard! So, let us try to keep this very basic and simple. God has three parts: body, soul, and spirit. If you believe anything else, then you are worshiping a different god than the one found in the King James Bible. Some Trinitarians believe in a god that consists of three persons, each with their own body, soul, and spirit. Thus, there would be NINE total parts to the Trinity. (Of course, there is no scripture for that.) Many other Trinitarians believe that God the Father and the Holy Ghost are both "spirit beings", while Jesus has his own body, soul, and spirit. So, I guess that version of the Trinity would have 5 parts in total? Again, no scripture for this position.

The other big problem for 5-part, or 9-part Trinitarians, is that James 3:9 plainly says that "men" are made after the "similitude of God." We are NOT God, but we are similar in our physical/ spiritual construction. God has three parts in his one person, and man is made the exact same way. How do we know this? Look at the verse below:

1 Thessalonians 5:23 And the very God of peace sanctify you wholly; and I pray God **your whole spirit and soul and body** be preserved blameless unto the coming of our Lord Jesus Christ.

There you have it, spelled out in plain English. The only way to miss this simple truth, is if you have been spoiled by philosophy. God has a spirit, soul, and body. Man has a spirit, soul, and body. Man is made after the similitude of God. If God has 5 or 9 parts, or if God is three separate persons, then man is not made after his similitude. Why is this so hard for Trinitarian hereticks to figure out?

But, what about Modalists? Do they believe that God and man both consist of three parts? No. In fact, Modalism is a teaching that God has a body, and the soul and spirit are basically the same thing. So, their God is not three parts, but two. This way they can say that Jesus the body was "God on earth", and God the Father, was the spiritual God in eternity. That is how they describe the distinction between God the Father and Jesus the Son. The Holy Spirit is merely symbolic of the "love" between the Father and the Son. You might be wondering where the Modalists came up with such an insanely heretical doctrine. Let me show you what the Catholic church teaches!

"A. CREATION

48. What is man?

Man is a creature composed of body and soul, and made to the image and likeness of God.

49. Is this likeness to God in the body or in the soul?

This likeness to God is chiefly in the soul.

The likeness to the Blessed Trinity is found chiefly in man's soul, but there is a resemblance in the body too-not, however, in the body of one man alone, but in man and woman united in marriage and the child which is the normal fruit of the marriage.

"God created man in his image. In the image of God He created him. Male and female He created them. Then God blessed them and said to them, "Be fruitful and multiply" (Gen. 1,27-28)

However, the image is found chiefly in man's soul, since that is a spirit just as God is a spirit."

(The New Saint Joseph Baltimore Catechism. Page 31)

This is another one of the very strange heresies taught by the Catholic church. Here is how it works: "God the Father and God the Son in eternity past looked on each other with love, and the love was so strong that it created the Holy Spirit." These papists will compare a marriage between a man and a woman, to this relationship of God the Father and the Son. The "fruit" of intimacy in marriage is a child, whereas the "fruit" of the intimacy between the Father and the Son, is the Holy Spirit. How in the world does that work? How can two males produce any fruit, through love? They cannot! Could this be the reason why there is so much pedophilia between Catholic boys and the Priests whom they call "Father"? It is truly disgusting!

Yet, in this very perverse and heretical teaching, we can see where Modalism comes from. They believe in a slightly altered version, but the basics are the same: One God who consists of two parts. Namely the body and the soul. The spirit comes from the love and interaction of the soul and the body. God on earth is Jesus, then he morphs into the Father when he shows up in heaven.

So, what have we learned so far? The Trinity teaching, and Modalism, both originate from the same source. Both false positions can be traced back to the Roman Catholic church. Neither position resembles the Godhead found in scripture. Trinitarians must add to the scriptures for their system to work, and Modalists must add and subtract from the scriptures to make sense of their system. God wants people to understand him on a very simple and basic level. God wants all of us to know that he created us in his image. We are all made after his similitude.

You and I both have a body, a soul, and a spirit. Before salvation, we were in a corruptible body of flesh, that loved to sin. Our soul was dark, and our spirit was dead. When God saves us, his holy Spirit moves into our bodies, and quickens our spirit (Ephesians 2:1-3). This, in turn, makes our soul become born again, and we are given a new life. Our body remains corruptible, but God's Holy Spirit helps us to fight against the sins that once tempted us and held us as prisoners. We no longer have any excuses to live in unrepentant sin (Romans 6:1-23)! The best part is, that we have a promise for a future resurrection, when God will, "change our vile body, that it may be fashioned like unto his glorious body." (See Philippians 3:20-21.) I cannot wait for that day!

Chapter 13: The Angel Of The Lord

Acts 27:23 For there stood by me this night **the angel of God**, whose I am, and whom I serve,

Here we have one of the clearest verses in the King James Bible, that proves just who the "angel of God" is. He is the one who owns Paul: "whose I am". He is also the one whom Paul serves: "whom I serve." Who was the apostle Paul serving during all of those years?

2 Timothy 1:3 I thank **God, whom I serve from my forefathers** with pure conscience, that without ceasing I have remembrance of thee in my prayers night and day;

Now, here is a very interesting truth: How could Paul serve God from his forefathers, if he was originally rejecting Jesus Christ before Acts Chapter 9? Paul was serving God the Father as a lost Pharisee, but he did not realize that Jesus Christ and the Father were the same being! Turn to the account of Paul on the road to Damascus in Acts Chapter 9. Begin reading at verse 3. Paul sees, "a light from heaven" that shone round about him. In verse 4, he hears a voice saying: "Saul, Saul why persecutest thou me?" And what is Paul's reply? He does not simply ask, "Who or what are you?" Paul knows he is dealing with God, because he sees his glory in verse 3. No angel, or other being, can manifest such a bright light!

Paul asks, "Who art thou, LORD"? Again, we must examine why Paul said it this way. Paul saw the glory of God, but he admits his lost condition, and openly confesses that the voice which he is hearing is a "Lord" that he himself does not know personally. Just like most Trinitarians, Paul had an intellectual understanding of who God is, but he could not make the connection that Jesus Christ is the Lord of heaven and earth! Jesus clears everything up for him when he says, "...I am Jesus whom thou persecutest...". What is Paul's reaction? Does Paul make a distinction between God the Father and Jesus the Son? No! Paul answers back, "Lord, what wilt thou have me to do?" in verse 6. Paul clearly shows that Jesus and the Father are one being, that can both be referred to as "Lord". Now, let us look at yet another passage where the apostle Paul clearly shows who the angel of God is:

Galatians 4:14 And my temptation which was in my flesh ye despised not, nor rejected; but received me as **an angel of God, even as Christ Jesus.**

Remember, the perfect wording of our King James Bible is all that is needed to define what words mean in their proper context. Whenever you read "even as", you know you are having a word or statement being defined as similar to whatever follows. So, in the above scripture, we have "an angel of God" followed by the statement, "EVEN AS". These two words are defining what an "angel of God" means. In context, an "angel of God" is the same thing as "Christ Jesus". Compare this to the statements Paul made in Acts 27:23, and you will see that it all lines up perfectly. But, before we move on to the next passage, we need to look at another Old Testament passage that proves who the angel of God is. It is found in Judges Chapter 13.

Judges 13:21 But **the angel of the LORD** did no more appear to Manoah and to his wife. Then Manoah knew that he was **an angel of the LORD**.

Judges 13:22 And Manoah said unto his wife, We shall surely die, because **we have seen God.**

Here, we see that the text says, "the angel of the Lord", which is obviously the same thing as the angel of God. But, look at Manoah's statement: "...we have seen God." This passage leaves no doubt that the angel of God (or the angel of the Lord) is a physical appearance of the Lord Jesus Christ! Please notice also, that Jesus shows up in a physical manifestation both before, and after, he came to the earth to die on the cross. Manoah saw Jesus in the Old Testament, and Paul saw Jesus in the New Testament, after his death, burial, and resurrection. Jesus is God. Do not forget it!

Chapter 14: God In His Eternal Future

Revelation 22:1 And he shewed me a pure river of water of life, clear as crystal, proceeding out of **the throne of God and of the Lamb**.

Revelation 22:2 In the midst of the street of it, and on either side of the river, *was there* the tree of life, which bare twelve *manner of* fruits, *and* yielded her fruit every month: and the leaves of the tree *were* for the healing of the nations.

Revelation 22:3 And there shall be no more curse: but **the throne of God and of the Lamb** shall be in it; and his servants shall **serve him**:

Revelation 22:4 And **they shall see his face**; and **his name** *shall be* in their foreheads.

Revelation 22:5 And there shall be no night there; and they need no candle, neither light of the sun; for **the Lord God giveth them light**: and they shall reign for ever and ever.

At the very end of the Bible, we see two names mentioned: 1. God and 2. the Lamb. Now, this is either two separate persons, or the same being with two different titles. If it is a reference to God the Father and "God the Son" (as the Trinity heresy states!), then why don't we see more than one "throne"? Shouldn't the text read something such as, "the thrones of God and of the Lamb"? Yet, there is only one throne. Why? Because there is only one person present, named God. There is no need for another throne.

Now, notice that verse 4 says that the saved will "see his face". Whose face? God, or the Lamb? The wording is clearly singular, and not plural. "His face" instead of "their faces". Again, we see another singular reference to this being in heaven. Please compare this to the fact that 2 Corinthians 4:6 speaks of, "...the glory of God in the FACE of Jesus Christ." Hebrews 1:3 says that Jesus is the "express image" of the person of God the Father. So, in eternity, the saved will be looking at the face of a being who is both God and the Lamb. One face. One God.

Verse 4 gives another confirmation of there being only one person named God. The verse says "his name". If you are a Trinitarian, I must ask you which name will be in "their foreheads"? God the Father, or the Son of God, known in context as the Lamb of God? "His name" is singular, and not plural. Please remember the simple statement: "Jesus is God". That is what I believe. If you believe something else, then please do not pretend that you are saved, because you are clearly LOST!

Then to really seal things, Revelation 22:5 says, "the Lord God giveth them light." Who is this referring to? The Father, or the Son? Turn back to Revelation Chapter 21, and look at this verse:

> **Revelation 21:22** And I saw no temple therein: for the Lord God Almighty and the Lamb are the temple of it.
>
> **Revelation 21:23** And the city had no need of the sun, neither of the moon, to shine in it: for **the glory of God did lighten it, and the Lamb is the light thereof.**

So, who is the one which gives the light in Revelation 22:5? Simple: The Lord God. The Bible teaches that Jesus is the light which produces the "glory of God." Remember that Jesus called himself, "the light of the world" in John 8:12. Ephesians 5:14 says to "...arise from the dead, and Christ shall give thee light." Jesus is also called the "Sun of righteousness" in Malachi 4:2. Interesting, because Paul said the light which shone round about him when he met Jesus on the road to Damascus, was, "above the brightness of the SUN." (Acts 26:13) Are you understanding this, yet? Jesus is not a lesser God than the Father. There are not "three persons" in heaven. There is only ONE God, and his name is Jesus.

Section 3: Common Trinitarian Attacks On Jesus

Chapter 15: Did Jesus Talk To Himself?

Matthew 26:39 And he went a little further, and fell on his face, **and prayed, saying, O my Father**, if it be possible, let this cup pass from me: nevertheless not as I will, but as thou wilt.

Now, as we enter into the final section of this book, we will begin to examine the common attacks which I have heard over the years, from Trinitarians which deny the Godhead doctrine. This argument is one of their favorites. They will smugly say something such as, "If Jesus is God the Father, does that mean that Jesus talked to himself?" I have even heard some Trinitarians mockingly say that perhaps your "Jesus" is schizophrenic. The funny thing is, that by using this as an argument against the Godhead doctrine, they are actually showing their ignorance of one of the most basic truths for a born-again Christian. Look at this verse:

Ephesians 5:19 Speaking to yourselves in psalms and hymns and spiritual songs, singing and making melody in your heart to the Lord;

All truly saved Christians TALK to themselves! Why? Because the word of God commands us to. Jesus was showing us how we should live in this world. All of us have a corruptible body of flesh that is prone to sin. Jesus never sinned, but he was tempted (Matthew 4:1). There are times that your soul needs to hear your flesh speaking, "psalms and hymns and spiritual songs." I can tell you that one of the quickest ways to destroy lust, is to start singing praises to Jesus Christ. If your flesh begins to fear men, start singing praises to God. Your soul needs to hear it! I wonder why Trinitarians do not understand this?

But, for the sake of the argument, let us consider the Trinitarian interpretation of Matthew 26:39. Jesus as "God the Son" was praying to a separate person known as "God the Father" in heaven. Why would he do that? Because God the Father could not possibly understand what Jesus the Son was going through. The love of a Father for his Son was there, but that was the only connection, if you believe in a Trinity. The SOUL of God was not suffering, in the Trinity system. Unless it was the soul of Jesus, exclusive of the soul of the Father. Do you see the mess the Trinity teaching makes of the Godhead doctrine of scripture? There is not one verse in the King James Bible which ever uses the word "persons" in relation to God.

Chapter 16: Was Jesus A Ventriloquist?

Matthew 3:17 And lo **a voice from heaven, saying, This is my beloved Son,** in whom I am well pleased.

Here is another attack which I have heard Trinitarian preachers use to mock the Biblical Godhead. They will refer to the baptism of Jesus, when God the Father speaks from heaven. Then they will say, "If Jesus is the same being as God the Father, was he speaking like a Ventriloquist?" Again, this is just another absurd attack on the Lord from Trinitarians, which shows their complete ignorance of scripture. The answer to their attack is, of course, very simple: Can a soul speak, when it is apart from its body? Read Revelation 6:9-11, and you will see the answer is a definite YES.

Now let us examine the context of Mathew Chapter 3, where the baptism of Jesus Christ happens. Look at verse 16. Please take note that EVERY written account of when Jesus was baptized, says that the Holy Spirit descended, "LIKE a dove". In other words, the Spirit of God floated down the same way a dove would fly to the ground. The Bible does not teach that the Holy Spirit is a bird! That heresy is another false teaching which has been propagated by the Catholic church.

The voice from heaven is clearly the soul of the Godhead, speaking about the event which is taking place on the earth. Much the same way as the souls of the martyrs are speaking in Revelation Chapter 6:9-11, and asking God to avenge their PHYSICAL blood which was shed on the earth. If you want further proof of this, then consider what Ephesians Chapter 2 teaches:

Ephesians 2:6 And hath raised us up together, and made us **sit together in heavenly places in Christ Jesus:**

Colossians 2:11 In whom also ye are circumcised with **the circumcision made without hands, in putting off the body of the sins of the flesh by the circumcision of Christ:**

Colossians 2:12 Buried with him in baptism, wherein also ye are risen with him through the faith of **the operation of God**, who hath raised him from the dead.

Now, here is a truly amazing fact: When God saves you, he performs an operation inside your body. He "circumcises" your sinful flesh, and cuts it free from your eternal soul. So, what you do in your sinful flesh will not affect your soul. This, of course, does not give you freedom to sin, because we know that the wages of sin is death (Romans 6:23). The Bible also says: "For if ye live after the flesh, ye shall die: but if ye through the Spirit do mortify the deeds of the body, ye shall live." (Romans 8:13)

So, then the question must be asked: If our soul is not connected to our sinful body of flesh, then where is the soul? This is what Ephesians 2:6 is describing. How could Jesus be walking around physically on the earth, and yet his soul is connected to eternity? The same way that we do today, if you are truly saved. The Bible teaches that we are members of Christ's body (Ephesians 5:30). How does this work, when we are clearly not connected to anything in a physical sense? Simple. It is our soul which was circumcised from our corruptible flesh, that now sits in heaven in perfect union with the Lord. Our soul is the spiritual connection, and the Spirit is the power which guides us into all truth.

Chapter 17: God In Three Persons?

Hebrews 1:3a Who being the brightness of his glory, and the express image of **his person**...

Before we answer this attack on Jesus, I feel a need to define the two words: "person" and "persons" for the Trinitarians which cannot seem to understand simple English. The word "person" is always a reference to a single individual or being. One man, and not many men. The word "persons" is always a reference to MORE than one man. Hopefully all rational PERSONS will agree with me on this well established fact. If you are part of the modern satanic "woke" movement (formally known as "politically correct" speech), then you are not part of what should be called "rational persons". People that want to eliminate "personal pronouns" and change the English language, so as not to upset perverts and other deviants, are not to be taken seriously.

Now we will take a few moments to list all references to the word "persons" in the King James Bible, and see how many times God is referred to as "persons":

Genesis 14:21 says, "Give me the **persons**". (Not a reference to God)

Genesis 36:6 says, "...all the **persons** of his house..." (Not a reference to God)

Exodus 16:16 says, "...according to the number of your **persons**..." (Not a reference to God)

Leviticus 27:2 says, "...the **persons** shall be for the Lord..." (Not a reference to God)

Numbers 19:18 says, ...upon the **persons** that were there..." (Not a reference to God)

Numbers 31:28 says, "...both of the **persons**..." (Not a reference to God)

Numbers 31:30 says, "...take one portion of fifty, of the **persons**..." (Not a reference to God)

Numbers 31:35 says, "...thirty and two thousand **persons** in all..." (Not a reference to God)

Numbers 31:40 says, "...the **persons** were sixteen thousand..." (Not a reference to God)

Numbers 31:40 says, "...the LORD'S tribute was thirty and two **persons**." (Not a reference to God)

Numbers 31:46 says, "And sixteen thousand **persons**;)" (Not a reference to God)

Deuteronomy 1:17 says, "Ye shall not respect **persons** in judgment..." (Not a reference to God)

Deuteronomy 10:17 says, "...which regardeth not **persons**..." (Not a reference to God)

Deuteronomy 10:22 says, "...with threescore and ten **persons**..." (Not a reference to God)

Deuteronomy 16:19 says, "...thou shalt not respect **persons**..." (Not a reference to God)

Judges 9:2 says, "...which are threescore and ten **persons**..." (Not a reference to God)

Judges 9:4 says, "...Abimelech hired vain and light **persons**..." (Not a reference to God)

Judges 9:5 says, "...being threescore and ten **persons**..." (Not a reference to God)

Judges 9:18 says, "...threescore and ten **persons**..." (Not a reference to God)

Judges 20:39 says, "...the men of Israel about thirty **persons**..." (Not a reference to God)

1 Samuel 9:22 says, "...which were about thirty **persons**." (Not a reference to God)

1 Samuel 22:18 says, "...slew on that day fourscore and five **persons**... (Not a reference to God)

1 Samuel 22:22 says, "...all the **persons** of thy father's house." (Not a reference to God)

2 Kings 10:6 says, "...Now the king's sons, being seventy **persons**..." (Not a reference to God)

2 Kings 10:7 says, "...slew seventy **persons**..." (Not a reference to God)

2 Chronicles 19:7 says, "...nor respect of **persons**, nor taking of gifts." (Not a reference to God)

Job 13:10 says, "...if ye do secretly accept **persons**." (Not a reference to God)

Job 34:19 says, "...accepteth not the **persons** of princes..." (Not a reference to God)

Psalms 26:4 says, "I have not sat with vain **persons**..." (Not a reference to God)

Psalms 82:2 says, "...accept the **persons** of the wicked?" (Not a reference to God)

Proverbs 12:11 says, "...he that followeth vain **persons**..." (Not a reference to God)

Proverbs 24:23 says, "...respect of **persons** in judgment." (Not a reference to God)

Proverbs 28:19 says, "...he that followeth after vain **persons**..." (Not a reference to God)

Proverbs 28:21 says, "To have respect of **persons** is not good..." (Not a reference to God)

Jeremiah 52:29 says, "...eight hundred thirty and two **persons**:" (Not a reference to God)

Jeremiah 52:30 says, "...seven hundred forty and five **persons**..." (Not a reference to God)

Jeremiah 52:30 Says, "...the **persons** were four thousand and six hundred." (Not a reference to God)

Lamentations 4:16 says, "...respected not the **persons** of the priests..." (Not a reference to God)

Ezekiel 17:17 says, "...to cut off many **persons**:" (Not a reference to God)

Ezekiel 27:13 says, "...they traded the **persons** of men..." (Not a reference to God)

Jonah 4:11 says, "...more than sixscore thousand **persons**..." (Not a reference to God)

Zephaniah 3:4 says, "Her prophets are light and treacherous **persons**..." (Not a reference to God)

Malachi 1:9 says, "...will he regard your **persons**?" (Not a reference to God)

Luke 15:7 says, "...over ninety and nine just **persons**..." (Not a reference to God)

Acts 10:34 says, "...God is no respecter of **persons**:" (Not a reference to God)

Acts 17:17 says, "...with the devout **persons**..." (Not a reference to God)

Romans 2:11 says, "For there is no respect of **persons** with God." (Not a reference to God)

2 Corinthians 1:11 says, "...by the means of many **persons**..." (Not a reference to God)

Ephesians 6:9 says, "...neither is there respect of **persons** with him." (Not a reference to God)

Colossians 3:25 says, "...and there is no respect of **persons**." (Not a reference to God)

1 Timothy 1:10 says, "...for perjured **persons**..." (Not a reference to God)

James 2:1 says, "...with respect of **persons**." (Not a reference to God)

James 2:9 says, "But if ye have respect to **persons**, ye commit sin..." (Not a reference to God)

1 Peter 1:17 says, "...the Father, who without respect of **persons**..." (Not a reference to God)

2 Peter 3:11 says, "...what manner of **persons** ought ye to be..." (Not a reference to God)

Jude 1:16 says, "...having men's **persons** in admiration..." (Not a reference to God)

Why would I take the time to type out over 50 references in the King James Bible to the word "persons"? Because it is very important for you, the reader of this book, to see that Trinitarians will lie right to your face! Their whole false teaching rests on their "God" consisting of three separate "persons". Without that, the doctrine of the Trinity completely falls apart.

Of course, the Trinitarians will say that the word "persons" might not be exactly spelled out in scripture, but the concept is there....somewhere. They will then take you through various scriptures to try and get you right back to the starting point of this Chapter: "God in three persons". They cannot survive without that! Every Trinitarian must add to the scriptures in order for their system to work. When they do this, just remind them of this verse:

Proverbs 30:6 Add thou not unto his words, lest he reprove thee, and **thou be found a liar**.

But, I want you to think about something else. If you look at the references to the word "persons" in the King James Bible, you will notice that nearly 20 times the scriptures warn about having "respect of persons". Ephesians 6:9 plainly states, "...your Master also is in heaven; neither is there **respect of persons** with him." Now compare that to Colossians 1:18, where the Bible says that Jesus is supposed to have "preeminence" in all things. Wouldn't that mean that God the Father is having "respect of persons" for his Son? The Trinity says that Jesus and the Father are two separate "persons", so if the Father glorifies anyone over himself, then he would be having "respect of persons", and would, therefore, be guilty of sinning (James 2:9). Are you still clinging to the Trinity? I certainly hope not!

Chapter 18: My Father Is Greater Than I

John 14:28 Ye have heard how I said unto you, I go away, and come again unto you. If ye loved me, ye would rejoice, because I said, I go unto the Father: **for my Father is greater than I.**

This attack is so easy to answer. It is more of an insult to any sane, rational mind to use this verse to attack Jesus. So, how could the Father be "greater" than Jesus, if they are the same person or being? Simple. Is a corruptible body of flesh greater, or worse, than an eternal soul? Worse. Obviously. Our bodies feel pain, grow older, need food everyday, must be exercised, need plenty of rest, and can be tempted to sin. What about our souls? Do our eternal souls feel or experience any of the above mentioned issues? No. So, it logically follows that anyone could make the statement that "my soul is greater than I".

But, let us stick with this Trinitarian philosophy for a minute. Alright, you (the Trinitarian) believe that Jesus is saying that the "person" of God the Father is greater than the "person" of "God the Son". How and why is the Father greater than the Son? (Please provide scriptures, of course!) What about 1 Timothy 6:14-15, where the Lord Jesus Christ is called, "the blessed and only Potentate, the King of kings, and Lord of lords." If Jesus is the only "Potentate", then where does that leave God the Father and the Holy Spirit? And, what do you do with these verses:

Isaiah 44:8 Fear ye not, neither be afraid: have not I told thee from that time, and have declared it? ye are even my witnesses. **Is there a God beside me? yea, there is no God; I know not any.**

Isaiah 43:11 I, even I, am the LORD; and **beside me there is no**

saviour.

Isaiah 45:21 Tell ye, and bring them near; yea, let them take counsel together: who hath declared this from ancient time? who hath told it from that time? have not I the LORD? and **there is no God else beside me; a just God and a Saviour; there is none beside me.**

Hosea 13:4 Yet I am the LORD thy God from the land of Egypt, and thou shalt know no god but me: for **there is no saviour beside me**.

Is God the Father greater than Jesus Christ? Yes. Is a soul greater than a physical body? Yes. Man is made after the similitude of God. Is your soul greater than your physical body? Yes. I should hope that this would be an obviously true statement. It would be insane to argue that the body is greater than the soul. That is all Jesus was saying in John 14:28. Jesus was not trying to teach that he and the Father are two separate persons. That is heretical nonsense!

Chapter 19: Jesus Seated At The Right Hand Of The Father

Hebrews 1:3 Who being the brightness of his glory, and the express image of his person, and upholding all things by the word of his power, when he had by himself purged our sins, **sat down on the right hand of the Majesty on high;**

Here we have another favorite attack on the Godhead, by Trinitarians. (It always amazes me how these people claim to love Jesus, while searching through the scriptures for anything that they can use to knock Jesus down to a lower position in heaven! Seems a little strange to me.) So, here is how this attack works: If Jesus and the Father are the same person, then how could the Son be seated on the right hand of the Father? Wouldn't this mean that they are two separate persons? I will answer this as we continue, but I need to remind you, the reader, that whenever anyone creates more than one person in God, you end up making a lot of serious doctrinal errors. Please never forget that. There is only one God, consisting of three parts: body, soul, and spirit.

The simple solution to Hebrews 1:3 is found a few verses later in verse 13 of the same Chapter. Please turn in your King James Bible, and actually read the entire context. Notice the defining word, "until" in verse 13. There is a future event that will end the task which Jesus is performing, by sitting at the right hand of the Father. What is this task? That would be Jesus ruling and reigning on the earth for 1,000 years. This prophecy is clearly laid out in Psalm 2, verses 7-12. Jesus will be fulfilling this in his PHYSICAL body. So, he will have a similar set up to how he walked on the earth the first time. His body was on the earth, and his soul was connected to his body, but in heaven as well. There is a separation there, but it is certainly NOT two separate "persons". (Please also compare this to the souls in Revelation 6:9-11, who are told to rest UNTIL their brethren are killed. The souls of the martyrs were separated from their bodies, UNTIL a future event unfolded. The same thing applies to Jesus and the Father.)

Now, let us read through some of the verses in the book of Hebrews Chapter 1. Start reading at verse 3. Notice that the Son (verse 2) is called, "the express image of his person." Jesus is the physical body of God, the Father is the soul, and the Holy Ghost is the spirit. That is the only way for the above statement to make sense. If you remember Chapter 7 where we discussed Genesis 1:26-27, we see the exact same word used to describe God: "image". Now, if you believe the King James Bible as it is written, you will understand that there is no way to teach multiple or different "images" with the Godhead. The Bible never teaches plural images for God. The Bible never teaches plural "persons" in God. If you deny this, then you are denying God's written word.

The rest of Hebrews 1:3 speaks of the prophetic nature of Jesus sitting at the right hand of the Father, until Jesus rules on the earth for 1,000 years. Verse 4 speaks of the inheritance which is promised to Jesus in Psalm 2. (On a side note, the ONLY proper view of the future, is the "Pre-Millennial" system of interpretation. Both the Amillennial and Post-Millennial systems rob Jesus of his promised earthly kingdom. Run away from anyone who is against the Pre-Millennial system!)

Now look at verse 5, and you will see some very interesting wording. Notice that God the Father says, "I will be to him a Father, and he shall be to me a Son." When have you ever heard a normal, mortal man make a statement like this? I never have. If a man is going to have a son, then he must obviously be the son's father. Yet, with God there is a different situation. The Godhead needed to consider what roles they would be playing in the redemption of man. That is why the soul of God says, "I will be to him a Father", and the body of God is made into the Son.

Verses 6-7 speak about the Father bringing Jesus his only begotten Son into the world, and also the relationship of Jesus with the other angels. But verse 8 contains an extremely unique phrase, in light of the topic of this book. Please notice in context that the verse is speaking about God the Father, and the verse says, "But unto the Son he saith, Thy throne, O God is for ever: a sceptre of righteousness is the sceptre of thy kingdom." First, we need to see the two singular references to: "Thy throne" and "thy kingdom". There are not two different thrones in heaven. There is only one throne. (Read through Revelation Chapter 4 and 5, and look at all of the singular references to "a throne" or "the throne", even though Jesus the lamb and God the Father are separate during these two Chapters.

Next, we must consider the most important part of Hebrews 1:8. Notice that God the Father says to Jesus, "Thy throne, O God is for ever and ever." He doesn't call Jesus "God number two", or "lesser God", or "other God". The Father worships the Son as "God". Why? Because Jesus is God. I truly hope that you have been assured of this fact, by now. The Father and Son are the same being, known as God.

Chapter 20: Jesus Delivers Up The Kingdom To The Father

1 Corinthians 15:24 Then cometh the end, when **he shall have delivered up the kingdom to God, even the Father**; when he shall have put down all rule and all authority and power.

In light of the previous Chapter, gaining an understanding of this Chapter should not be very difficult for a serious student of God's Holy written word. Turn in your King James Bible to 1 Corinthians 15, and begin reading at verse 21. Here we have a description of the future for redeemed saints. The resurrection of all those who died in Christ, is one of the greatest promises found in scripture. Verse 22 shows our corruptible seed inherited through Adam, and our incorruptible seed inherited through Christ. Verse 23 shows the order of the different parts of the resurrection. First we have those Old Testament saints (firstfruits) who came up after Jesus rose from the dead (Matthew 27:52-53). Next, are those whom belong to Christ: that would be the Christian church (2 Corinthians 10:7).

Verse 24 speaks of the end of the Millennial kingdom. This is when the rest of the dead are resurrected. (Read Revelation 20:5, which concludes what is called, "the first resurrection".) The first resurrection has three parts to it, and it is for the saved. The next "resurrection" is for the dead souls of all the lost who died and went to Hell, where they were waiting for their final judgment. Revelation 20:12-15 covers this other resurrection. No saved man or woman will be judged at the great white throne judgment. It is strictly a final judgment for the lost, before they are thrown into the lake of fire for all of eternity.

So, what happens after the resurrection of the just, and the unjust? (Acts 24:15) That is when the Son of God has completed his work on the earth, and he can deliver up the kingdom to his own eternal soul in heaven, known as God the Father. Then they become one, because the prophecies are finally fulfilled. The earth has been burned up (2 Peter 3:10), so there is no more need for, "... all rule and all authority and power" (1 Corinthians 15:24). Verse 25 prophecies that all enemies will be put under the feet of Jesus. This is a reference to the earth being the "footstool" of God in Matthew 5:35. Verses 26-27 go on to speak about how Jesus will conquer everything, including death itself.

Verse 28 says that all things will be, "subdued unto him", and that the Son also himself will be, "subject unto him that put all things under him...". Again, the Trinitarians will try to make this the person Jesus Christ being submissive to the separate person of God the Father. They willingly ignore the multitude of scriptural contradictions this would make, because they are so desperate to knock Jesus off of the throne. So, what does the verse really mean? The soul is the greater part of God that does not feel physical pain, and is eternal. The body of God must fulfill certain prophecies that will require pain, and other emotions, which the soul will not directly experience. When these physical prophecies are fulfilled, than the body and soul can join and rule as one being in heaven. How do we know this? Read the last part of the verse:

1 Corinthians 15:28 And when all things shall be subdued unto him, then shall the Son also himself be subject unto him that put all things under him, **that God may be all in all**.

When God is finally "all in all", then all the scriptures will have been fulfilled. God the Father, Jesus the Son, and the Holy Spirit will all be perfectly united in heaven, as ONE being. All the work of redemption is completed. All of the lost are in the lake of fire, with their father Satan. ALL of God's plans have been brought to pass, exactly as his written word said they would happen. The Lord Jesus Christ, Almighty God that he is, will rule and reign completely and without question. He will truly be worthy of ALL, "...power, and riches, and wisdom, and strength, and honour, and glory, and blessing." (Revelation 5:12).

Chapter 21: Three Spirits

Revelation 16:13 And I saw **three unclean spirits** like frogs come out of the mouth of the dragon, and out of the mouth of the beast, and out of the mouth of the false prophet.

Now, here we have a very interesting prophecy: Three separate "persons", with more than one "spirit" controlling them. If you want proof for a "Trinity", here it is! The problem, of course, is that this "Trinity" is composed of the three most evil beings in world history. Satan, the Antichrist, and the false prophet. They will literally be ruling on this earth as a physical, visible Trinity. Sadly, this is what most professing "Christians" are truly worshiping, when they talk about the three person Trinity. They are either completely ignorant of the Godhead issue, and just repeating the philosophical Trinitarian terms. Or, they are knowingly hating the true God of the Bible while claiming to be saved. It happens all the time. (Paul warned about "false brethren" in 2 Corinthians 11:26.)

Of course, the common Trinitarian answer to this, is that in order for Satan to make his own "Trinity", there must be a real "Trinity" in heaven for him to counterfeit. This, of course, is a ridiculous argument. Does Satan need a heavenly example of drugs, in order for him to counterfeit it, and make his "dangerous drugs" here on the earth? No, of course not. So, what is Satan really trying to accomplish by showing up as a "Trinity" on the earth, in the future? It is his favorite trick, which he has used for thousands of years to get God to judge people. Here is how it works: If Satan can form a false god, and get people to worship it instead of the Lord, then God will be forced to punish them! Very simple, but it works quite well. Let me demonstrate:

First, we have the garden of Eden. Satan gets Eve to worship her own intellect, in Genesis 3:5. This trick still works quite well among atheists in Academia. They usually fall for it, without questioning Satan, or checking to see what the Bible really says. The next trick Satan uses, if he cannot get through the intellect, is to send devils to pose as other gods. These devils become idols to the people, and require ritual sacrifices. (Read 1 Corinthians 10:19-20.) And, here is where Satan will often use confusing and contradicting terms to gain control of the people's minds. This is why I believe it was Satan who created the terms used in the Trinity. If that sounds like a radical statement, then I would like to remind you, the reader, that Trinitarian terminology has no basis in scripture. So, if God did not come up with it, then that leaves only one other possibility!

To further prove this point, we will quickly look at a few passages in scripture, where a single idol is referred to as "gods". In the following scriptures you will see that Satan has been working for thousands of years, to prepare people for his ultimate battle plan for the end times. Let us begin by turning in our King James Bibles to Exodus Chapter 32, and we will begin reading at verse 7. First, I must point out that, in context, we see God speaking to Moses. Now, notice the interesting contrasts between the singular and plural wording of verse 8.

Exodus 32:8 They have turned aside quickly out of the way which I commanded them: they have made them **a molten calf**, (singular) and have worshipped **it**, (singular) and have sacrificed thereunto, and said, These be thy **gods**, (plural) O Israel, which have brought thee up out of the land of Egypt.

Isn't that a strange thing for the Lord to see ONE "molten calf", and yet he quotes the people as calling it, "thy gods". Now, how can one calf be called multiple gods? Perhaps the children of Israel could have also called it, "God in three persons, blessed Trinity"? "God the Father, God the Son, and God the Holy Ghost. Three different Gods, but only one God." Utter nonsense! There is no scripture to defend this horrible Trinity teaching. If God hated what the children of Israel were doing with their false idol worship, I can promise you that God also hates the Trinity just as much. Stop adding to the scriptures, and repent of your false idols while there is still time.

1 Kings 18:21 And Elijah came unto all the people, and said, How long halt ye between two opinions? if the LORD be God, follow him: but if **Baal, then follow him**. (singular) And the people answered him not a word.

1 Kings 18:24 And **call ye on the name of your <u>gods</u>,** (plural) and I will call on the name of the LORD: and the God that answereth by fire, let him be God. And all the people answered and said, It is well spoken.

1 Kings 18:26 And they took the bullock which was given them, and **they dressed it, and called on the name of Baal** (singular) from morning even until noon, saying, **O Baal**, (singular) hear us. But there was no voice, nor any that answered. And they leaped upon the altar which was made.

Turn in your King James Bible to 1 Kings Chapter 18, and read the whole story of Elijah challenging the priests of Baal. Again, you will see a singular reference to the false god named, "Baal", and yet Elijah also says, "gods" in relation to the god Baal. Are we seeing yet another ancient example of pagan people worshiping a singular, yet plural, "god"? Yes, we certainly are! Now, let us look at one more example of false gods that form a Trinity:

Turn back to 1 Kings Chapter 11, and begin reading in verse 1. Notice that King Solomon's interracial marriage to non-Jewish women, caused him to turn after other "gods" (Verses 1-4). Now let us count the number of these false gods in verses 5-7: 1. Ashtoreth the goddess, 2. Milcom, 3. Chemosh, 4. Molech. The Trinitarian will quickly point out that there are FOUR false gods, and not three, thereby making it impossible to tie it into the Trinity. For those who would say this, you are only proving your ignorance of the ancient and modern false gods of lost heathens.

Please look again at the names of these four false gods, and you will see a very obvious Trinity: "Milcom, Chemosh, and Molech." There you can see the three "gods". But what about the female goddess known as, "Ashtoreth"? How does that line up with the modern day Trinity? Very simple. Look at a picture of the Roman Catholic Trinity, and you will often see FOUR beings present: "God the Father, God the Son, God the Holy Spirit (symbolized by the white dove), and Mary the Queen of Heaven / Mother of God." And there you have it. Modern pagan Catholics worshiping the same false idols that Solomon once worshiped. All they had to do was change the names a little, to deceive the masses into thinking that their false idols are somehow based in scripture.

I can promise you that this ancient "Trinity" concept, will be showing up in the future. Revelation Chapter 13 speaks very clearly about three separate beings: 1. The beast, 2. The dragon, and 3. the false prophet. You can be sure that Mary will also show up with her "immaculate heart", to convince the world that her son "Jesus" (in reality, the Antichrist!) must be worshiped without question! If saved Christians do not wake up to the false Trinitarian system, and openly denounce it as a pagan philosophy, they will be taking part in setting the stage for the satanic Trinity of the future, which will cause the damnation of most of the world's population. I thank the Lord for showing me the truth of the Godhead doctrine, and I, for one, will NEVER again teach or support the "Trinity" concept!

Conclusion

Now that we have come to the end of this book, I sincerely hope and pray that you have been convinced at just how great and powerful the Lord Jesus Christ truly is! Jesus is God. He always has been, and he always will be, God. The Godhead consists of the Father (soul), Son (body), and Holy Ghost (spirit). We are made after the similitude of God. We have a soul, a body, and a spirit. God is NOT three persons, and neither are we. Please do not let any philosopher take you away from the "simplicity that is in Christ." (2 Corinthians 11:3)

Did I answer every Trinitarian argument? No. Did I discuss every scripture which proves that Jesus Christ and God the Father are the same being? No. That was not the point of this book. The written word of God must be your authority, not my book. The King James Bible teaches the Godhead doctrine. The King James Bible never says, "Trinity", or "divine essence", or "God the Son", or "God the Spirit", or "three persons". NEVER compromise on that! God does not want the Trinity taught, because he never put it in his word. If a Trinitarian refuses to submit to the written word of God as their final authority, than part company with them. It is that simple.

The other thing I have learned over the years, is that even if you answer every objection given by an enemy of the Bible, they will just invent some new arguments to attack the truth. I have dealt with this for many years now. Trust me. If someone rejects the truth, you cannot help them by continuing to argue with them. The Holy Spirit will guide them into the truth, if they are genuinely born again. (John 16:13) Remember that "natural men" (lost people) cannot receive the truth, according to 1 Corinthians 2:12-14. The arguments presented in this book are the best to use when defending the Godhead doctrine. There are many others which the Lord will show you as you study the King James Bible on your own.

One final note I need to make, is the tremendous amount of

confusion which the Trinity and Modalism teachings have made among the lost world. I have been contacted over the years by both Jews and Muslims, who could not understand the contradictions of the Trinitarian system. They do not understand how Christians can claim that Jesus Christ is God, while claiming that he is a separate person from God the Father, and then they say that there is only ONE God. I can understand why they are confused! The Trinity makes zero sense to a logical mind.

The Christian Church MUST have the scriptures as our final authority. This book has proved that Trinitarianism and Modalism are false systems of belief. We cannot simply "agree to disagree" on this issue, with other professing Christians. If they reject the Godhead doctrine, then they are rejecting the Lord Jesus Christ. Never forget the stern warning which Jesus himself made:

John 8:24 I said therefore unto you, that ye shall die in your sins: for if ye believe not that I am he, ye shall die in your sins.